2013 Chokoloskee Island

Chokoloskee Island, Florida

Published in the United States of America

By

GBP

Grizzly **B**ookz **P**ublishing

A Not-For-Profit Organization

Proceeds from the sale of books

by

Rick Magers

are donated to the following.

The Smallwood Trading Post in Chokoloskee, Florida.

Katia Solomon, the girl in Ladybug and the Dragon.

Homeless animal caregivers, wherever we find them.

Books by this author: 2013

- Dark Caribbean
- The McKannahs
- The McKannahs ~ together again ~
- Carib Indian
- The Face Painter
- The Black Widowmaker
- Satan's Dark Angels
- America
- A Sacred Vow
- It's A Dog's Life
- 80 Stories
- Ladybug and the Dragon

All books by this author are available on his website or by contacting him by email. His books are available at Amazon and Barnes & Noble…and as eBooks also.

www.grizzlybookz.net

magersrick@yahoo.com

A description of each book is on the last page.

Ghosts

OF

Chokoloskee

A strange and eerie story

by

Rick Magers

(Using notes made by Pyorrhea Lam)

Many heart-felt thanks to my long-time friend,

Audrey Hamann. She critiques my books

with a talent that leaves no questions

in my mind that it will run past

the reader's eyes in a very

smooth way, whether

or not they

enjoy

it.

.

.

Dedication ~ TO ~ my friends

.

.

At

77 I am

extremely

lucky to have

so many good loyal

friends. Larry and Beth are

two that have been my friends for

decades. They have provided me with the

best place that a writer could ever hope to find.

Most of the ghosts in this story were real people that the author either knew while they were alive or knew their relatives, and spent time listening as they were described in detail—as much as the law will allow. Remember, this was not only a permanent oasis for hardy pioneers, but also a pit stop for an assortment of one-foot-over-the-line entrepreneurs, poachers, smugglers, and killers, along with other colorful individuals who ran close to the edge of life's precipice—unconcerned about the abrupt stop at the bottom.

If any of the fictional characters depicted in this book, alive or dead, remind you of yourself or someone you know or knew, it was purely unintentional, and the author apologizes—sorta.

~ death comes but once to all—enjoy the experience ~

PREFACE

I went on a trip to Key West a little over 60 years ago aboard a Trailways bus, or maybe it was a Greyhound? My memory, like other body parts, doesn't work as well these days. Most have been working hard for 77 years, so I guess that's understandable? But it still sucks. Hell, I mighta hitchhiked, for all I know?

Back to that delightful trip to the southernmost point in the continental USA. At that time I was living in Miami with my older brother, who, at only twenty-two and fresh out of college had landed a job with the Miami Herald as a sports reporter.

While Lenin (our parents were not commies. Hattie, our mom, simply liked that name) was struggling slowly up the newspaper ladder, I was busy writing small columns and articles about fishing and camping for any outdoors rag that I heard was publishing unknown writers. I considered myself pretty damn lucky, because I'd much rather fish and go camping than trudge off to some job that I hated every day, like most folks I know.

My dad, Elrod, helped me get a writing position on his friend's magazine, Florida's Great Outdoors, and my first column was titled Silver Bait-Bandits of the Ten Thousand Islands. Most Yankee tourists had never heard of the Florida Snook, even though famed author of western novels, Zane Grey, came often to Everglades City to fish for 'em, as did a couple of presidents and more than a few movie stars. And ole Zane even broke a few snook records. But by the 1950s many Yankees had already started coming to the west coast of Florida looking for something other than oranges, bathing beauties, and bumper-to-bumper traffic bimbos.

After a long dry period, several Florida publications and one national magazine were regularly buying my stories and articles about fishing the areas of the southwest coast of Florida from Naples to Flamingo. I was making enough money in 1960 to buy a houseboat from a guy in Miami who worked for an aluminum outfit, and built the aluminum boat in his Hialeah back yard.

I stopped by to see a fella that I knew named Gunn, who built Gunn's boatyard on the Miami River up near the dam-pins close to Hialeah. I told him that I was looking to buy a used houseboat that I could live aboard and cruise Florida's coastal waters to fish and write stories about my travels.

Turns out this guy who built the darn thing didn't discuss anything ever with his wife. His plan to retire from his three-car taxicab company, Maxi-Taxi, that he'd been working in ever since before they came equipped with turn signals, received a flat "NO" from his frumpy frau. Gunn said the guy tied the houseboat to his dock and asked him to sell it and keep 25% of whatever he got. "That thing's welded together as good as any aluni, alunim, alimin." Gunn stumbled over that difficult word a couple more times then said, "Aw nuts, as good as any lightmetal boat I ever saw."

He also told me that it had a small three cylinder Lister diesel attached to a three foot long shaft with universal joints, to a commercial grade outdrive that pushed the houseboat along at fifteen knots while only turning two thousand or so RPMs.

"That little diesel oughta still be running after you and me are dead n' buried, Pyorrhea." Yes, that's my name, Pyorrhea Lam. My friends call me Py and let it go at that. I never changed it for the same reason Lenin didn't. We loved Hattie, so whatever she wanted was okay by us.

Gunn and I went up the ladder so I could see the inside. He had pulled it up outa the Miami River and set the boat on a carriage so it would be safe from the vandals that preyed on easy targets by cruising along in little boats with small quiet motors. After his two well-trained Rottweilers had re-sized two thieves who climbed the fence, and went right over his warning sign, nobody ever tried sneaking in after that.

"The judge," Gunn said, "told them both that they were lucky to have made it to the dock so they could jump in the river, even though one came to the surface missing a hand and the other missing an eye." He told me later that they were both wanted in connection with a murder over on Miami Beach, and eventually were sent to Raiford, the Federal Pen in North Florida. They were both killed the first year.

Anyway, we climbed up and went inside. That guy's wife musta been a humdinger, because he was a real craftsman and went way overboard to make it extremely comfortable and nice inside. Ah well, takes all kinds. I'm sorta like a nun where those wives are concerned. Ain't got none, never wanted none, ain't gonna bring none home. I've had lots of girlfriends over the years that fell in love with this boat, so after enjoying their company for a while, I always gave each one a picture of it to remember me by, and sent 'em packing.

The thing that I like the most about this boat (in 2012 by the way, I'm still living and cruising on it) is the way he designed it like a canal boat that cruises the rivers over in Europe. Low profile so they can get under all those bridges.

The hull, deck, and cabin are all aluminum, and all of the welded seams are as good as any that I inspected while I was prowling 'Used Yachts' places along both Florida coasts looking for a Striker I could afford. Didn't take many stops to realize that I was not in a Striker income category—used or very used.

She's 36' long and 12' wide, and a nearly unbelievable 8' 4" from the 4 x 8 inch solid aluminum keel to the top of the roof, which is ¼" aluminum. The roof and ceiling are sandwiched on 3" aircraft trusses. It created a tough structural ceiling inside that is easy to keep clean, and when someone walks across the roof it doesn't ripple, wobble, or move.

The keel is welded to a 3 x 12 inch solid aluminum keelson. 3" square aluminum pipe is welded to it forming the ribs of the bottom, and the side ribs are welded to them. They're all on 24" centers. 3" square pipe also creates a chine and gunwale where the ribs are welded. ¼" (I'm gonna stop saying aluminum because the boat's all aluminum) sheet completes the sides, deck, and bottom. All are welded to ribs, making it rigid enough to feel comfortable beneath my feet when under power, but flexible enough to handle waves up to three feet.

By having an extremely shallow-draft vessel, I can go

in close to shore and hug the coastal beach or mangroves wherever I go, so when weather begins to deteriorate, I quickly move to a sheltered area and drop anchor. If I ever punch a hole in the bottom all I gotta do is have her hauled, and after the water drains out, patch the hole. The floor inside from stem to stern is welded tight, which created a double-bottom.

The decking on the bow is 36" from the nose to the cabin. Along both sides of the cabin and across behind the cabin is 20" wide. Since the cabin's top is only 3' above the deck I can move swiftly fore and aft by holding to the handrail running the distance of the cabin.

By using 6½" aircraft-type trusses welded to each rib across the bottom and then welding and riveting ¼" plate to create a floor and walls, the guy ended with a very low profile vessel and kept most of the weight down low.

Two things the builder did convinced me that he was much too bright an engineer to be driving a taxi. But Gunn knew him a long time and said he enjoyed being a cabbie, plus owning his own cabs let him make a good living.

The first thing I noticed was the spoon bow he put on the boat. From the outside it looked like it mighta been made of fiberglass, but not many people at that time were convinced that glass of any kind was gonna work on a boat, so I scrubbed that thought.

Gunn walked over after talking to a guy about hauling a boat out on his ways. "Pretty good job he did on that bow, huh?"

"Yeah," I replied, "didn't know what he used till I tapped on it."

Gunn said, "Aluni, uh alu, aw crap, lightmetal. Neat job the way he made each piece of lightmetal fit perfectly to the bow ribs he welded on before he began sheathing the nose." He bent down and pointed, "Look at this, Py. This spoon bow flows so darn smoothly into the rest of the bottom I thought at first that he musta used long strips a few inches wide."

"Wow, if it wasn't for the welding beads most folks would think it's one big chunk o' lightmetal." (I darn sure wasn't about to say aluminum and take the chance of making Gunn mad—at least not until I closed the deal)

"He told me he built a press to put a slight cup in each piece the narrow way so they'd all fit side-by-side." Gunn backed out and stood straight then rubbed his back. "I've done it with wood to make a bow look just right, but darned if I know how he did this."

Gunn ran a water hose to the engine, and when he started that little three-cylinder Lister diesel, the thing sounded like a sewing machine. The builder ran the exhaust through a muffler, and since it was a dry stack, he wrapped it all with a special asbestos material, and then covered it with a heavy gauge foil tape about 3" wide. Air scoops bring fresh air into the engine room, so it's never really hot in there, because stainless steel spinners on each corner of the roof pulls the hot air and fuel fumes out. The rear six feet of the boat is the engine room and fuel tanks. A little single-cylinder Lister diesel mounted to a 3 kw generator provides all the electricity I'll ever need, and it takes up about the same space that a couple of cases of beer would. Since I don't drink anything but water, coffee, and tea, then it wasn't taking up needed space.

After Gunn shut down the main engine, he opened the port on the one-lung Lister and turned the flywheel twice then let go. He then closed the port and that little beauty chugged away like a smaller version of that engine in the African Queen—chuk, achuk, chuk, achuk. When he threw a switch on the generator, a light on each side of the engine room lit the place like a Vegas casino. He pointed at a small power box on the wall, "Py, all of the hunert n' ten volt stuff is wired to the generator thru this here box." He pulled the cover open to show me. "That little Dometic camper fridge's on a separate breaker, 'cause 'at there," he pointed at the little Lister, "generator cain't handle but a few light bulbs when the fridge's on electric. Them two aluni, aleem, aw nuts, lightmetal propane bottles I showed you up on the cabin top will keep the fridge running cold for about four months, according to ole Maxi."

I'd already looked through the inside area and really liked the way it was set up, so I followed Gunn through the engine room door and along the narrow hall between the two staterooms. He went on through the galley to the wheelhouse. I had certainly already noticed the plush, padded, captain's chair and the big stainless steel steering wheel in front of it.

Gunn stepped aside and motioned with his chiseled chin for me to climb into the seat. "That's the most comfortable darn captain's chair I ever sat in," he said as I settled into it.

As I was looking over the panel of gauges, Gunn pressed a button on the front of the right armrest. The entire chair rose just like those barbershop chairs. "It goes up a foot," he said, "I stand six foot in socks, and I can see over the bow just fine, but when I sit in there n' run 'er up a foot, man oh man, they ain't nothin goin on out front that I don't see."

The only feature I had doubts about was the method of entering the boat's inner quarters. On the port side of the engine room section of the cabin is a sailboat type entry hatch. It's three feet wide by four feet long, so the main engine can be removed without cutting anything if it's ever necessary. It slides back on runners welded to the cabin top. Those runners are six inches high and allows rainwater to flow right past and onto the deck. The vertical door is 3 feet wide but only two and a half feet high, and since the cabin top is only three feet above the deck, then it's a six inch threshold to step over. This, plus the fact that the door and the track it slides up and out of is all recessed four inches in, which is sealed when the top is pulled back and locked, makes it almost waterproof.

The main entry is on top of the cabin, and might be why Maxi's bride nixed the entire project. Gunn said if a ponytail was tied to her dress in the back she could fill in for one of those Budweiser wagon haulers.

Gunn opened it from the inside to show me. The aluminum ladder rests against the ceiling and is 30" wide. He pulled a lever and the ladder began slowly coming down. "Y'gotta push it back up manually," he said, "but Maxi built in a hydraulic rig of some kind that allows the ladder to drop down slow." He turned to me and grinned, "Pretty dern smart for a taxi driver, huh?"

I pointed to a small box at the end that had screws to remove a cover, "That must be where the unit is if it ever needs work."

"Yeah, I reckon so," Gunn said. "I was always gonna open it to see what's in there, but never got around to it."

"It'll suit me fine," I said, "if I never hafta open it." The ladder was against the floor now, so I watched as Gunn went up the four inch wide steps a ways, and then swung the lever holding the hatch closed. As he went up he held a nylon rope that let the hatch cover go back slowly until it rested against the propane bottles' guardrail.

Two 40 pound propane bottles were mounted in a rack at the end of the entrance hatch, and they had a 30" rail around them that projected back three feet on each side of the hatch. Gunn held to it and stepped out onto the roof, so I did the same. "C'mere, Py." He was pointing at the end of the hatch, so I climbed on up and went around to see what it was.

"I brought the key with me." Gunn held up a heavy looking key, "Maxi gave me three spares too. Y'gotta lift this heavy rubber that covers the key hole, and then just shove the key in and turn it. Watch." He turned the key and a stainless half-inch diameter rod came out on both sides about an inch. "Them rods go into the housing the hatch sits on, and once the key's pulled out, they ain't gonna move. When you're inside all y'gotta do is turn the lever to make them rods come back into the hatch so you can push 'er up."

I'd never thought about it until Gunn told me that the guy did not think a boat builder should ever put a hole in the bottom of a boat unless he was trying to sink it. Gunn, being a boat yard man that was raised around boats that all had holes in the bottom for engine water, toilet water, deck wash-down hoses, etc., laughed. "Maxi's got ideas nobody else would even think about, but c'mere Py n' look at this." I followed him back into the engine room. "See this square lightmetal box stickin up next to the poophouse wall?" Gunn pointed at a box about a foot square and two feet high, which was welded all the way around the floor and up the sides against the bulkhead. I'd seen it while we were in there earlier but forgot to ask what it was.

"Yeah," I answered, "I figured it was the water intake, since those hoses go to both engines, but I've never seen anything quite like that."

"Well," Gunn said as he removed his Stetson. It really is a Stetson, too, because he showed me the label that's still in it. But I reckon ole man Stetson would have a fit n' roll over in his grave if he saw it. I once asked him about it because Gunn put it on in the morning and kept it on all day.

"M'aunt Hatty from up in Ocala went on a bus tour with her Bingo Biddies," he grinned and told me that was the name of her club, "and she won the darn thing playin bingo. Toted it all the way back from Arizona to give it to me. That was back in 60, and even then a Stetson cost more'n a set o' tires for m'goldang pickemup truck. I wore it like it was for months, but that wide brim kept hittin ever dang thing I got near, so I whacked it off."

He left about a half-inch brim all the way around. If he glued a red tassel in the middle he'd look like one of those Shriners in a parade.

He pulled his red kerchief from a pocket in his bib overalls and wiped the inside band and his forehead, then put the Stetson back on. "I been meanin t'hava look inside but been busy, so let's see what it looks like." I watched as

he loosened the clamps to pull the hoses off of the 1 ½"
pipes they were shoved down on. "These two are
seawater to the diesels, and this one goes to the pooper.
Them other three are spares," he pointed toward the three
pipes with no hose attached.

Gunn opened the latches on both ends of the cover
and lifted it off. He held it up to look closer at the three
other inner hoses attached to the same three pipes he'd
just removed the outer hoses from. "Look at these screen
shoes." He held the lid up so I could see the bronze intake
shoes clamped to the ends of the three hoses. "By golly,
Py, I ain't found anything yet that ole Maxi scrimped on.
These pickups are the best that money can buy." He
placed it on the floor and said, "Have a look, Py, these're
the holes in the bottom you asked about." I leaned over
and saw the half-inch holes in the bottom of the seawater
intake box. "I've never seen a better set up for water
intake," Gunn said. "Those dern thru-hull water intake
fittings on lotsa boats are too often in lousy places where
ya just can't get to the dern things." He shook his head as
he replaced the cover, and replaced the outer hoses. "I've
seen 'em down under the goldang engine, or up against a
bulkhead so tight y'can't hardly get to the clamp screw,
and when y'do, it ain't stainless and won't budge, so
y'gotta start cuttin hose n' sawin with a friggin hacksaw.
Or sometimes chiseling wood on a stringer 'cause some
jerk drilled the hole too close." He snugged up the clamps
and put the screwdriver back inside the toolbox. "Py, I've
come up outa the bilges so dang bloody after replacing a
thru-hull fitting, I musta looked like I needed a friggin
transfusion." He wiped his hatband again, "And all
because the doggone shore cord was plugged in wrong or

the wooden boat was docked next to a steel hull and all the fittings had been eaten up by electrolysis." He nodded at the intake box, "I gotta give ole Maxi credit for som'n like that. It juss now took me only a few minutes to check all the hoses. C'mon, let's go." He stopped at the ladder going up out of the engine room, "Lotta boats went to the bottom on account o' those crapper hoses was installed in a place so hard t'get to that nobody ever checks 'em till the boat's sinkin, and then it's usually too goldang late." Gunn went up and I followed.

The toilet and shower were both in one compartment, right between the engine room and the smaller stateroom. Gunn went around the corner and watched as I closed the hatch to the engine room. "I'll lock it," Gunn nodded toward the hatch, "when we go back inside, but look at this, Py." He pointed at a metal cap on the cabin just up off the deck. I watched as he removed it. "You asked about that tank in the top of the shower. Well, I wanted to show you this before explaining. No, it ain't the fresh water for the shower." He grinned, "You'll get one heckuva crappy shower if it ever ruptures. It's a chemical tank for the pooper, and remind me t'show ya where t'put in the chemical if ya decide to buy the boat. There's a two inch hose about twenty feet long that connects on here in case you ever hafta prove that you only dump the pooper at docks that have tanks. There's a good heavy duty twelve volt pump that'll empty this thirty gallon tank into a holding tank at a dock if y'ever have to. But there's a four footer that he puts on here when he's cruising," Gunn shook his head, "Maxi only cruised in this boat twice that I know of, and I went along with him both times. Once when we went out to Stiltsville off the end of Key Biscayne to spend the weekend, and a trip we took to Key Largo. On the way back, both times, we put on the short hose and pumped all the crap overboard. We never put paper in the toilet. He has a little trash can with a lid, and we line the can with a Wal-Mart bag. It's in the pooper, and that's where we put the paper, then later we tossed the plastic Wal-Mart shopping bag into a dumpster somewhere. That chemical works good too, because it's almost clear when it comes out and don't smell like poop." He turned and grinned, "I ain't gonna say it smells good, just don't smell like poop. Maxi only uses a little, because with no paper to break down, it doesn't take much to break down the poop enough so it'll go thru the pump's impeller."

I followed Gunn down the ladder and we went into his office on the front of the property, next to Northwest South River Drive. I had no idea at all what kinda money he hoped to get for it, so all I did was just wait for him to talk.

Finally he said, "Well Py, whadaya think?"

"About what, Gunn?"

"The goldang boat, fer cryin out loud, whadaya think? About the frigin price o' mullet?"

"I like the boat alright, Gunn, but I ain't a rich author like m'brother, Lenin."

"Well, Py, I ain't gonna bullcrap ya. That thing has been sittin there for dang near a year, and ain't been one person that seemed interested. I reckon everybody wants one of the conventional type boats," he laughed, "and that boat's not gonna fit into any conventional category."

He leaned back in his chair and looked real hard at me for about five minutes while he chewed on a matchstick, but I didn't say squat. I just sat there lookin around his walls at all the fish he'd caught over the years and had his friend, Pflueger, stuff for him.

"I wanna get that oddball boat outa here, Py, and you're the only goldang bohunk I know that don't give a rat's ass what other people say." Gunn remained quiet for about two more minutes, and then said, "Gimme twenty thousand cash, and I'll put new RotoMetal twenty-four inch zincs on her and have the boys put a new paint job on the entire hull with the same stuff that the guys use on those alemu, alulu, doggonit, lightmetal Strikers."

~ O ~

Two weeks later I was heading down the Miami River towards Biscayne Bay in my new boat. New to me, but actually she was about as new as boats go, because I think those two trips were all the boat ever made. Gunn told me that if a person designed a boat just like it and had him build it, the price would be near a hundred thousand. That was back in 1960, so I reckon I was in the right place at the right time with enough dough to swing the deal. I've been living on it and cruising Florida's coastal waters ever since and even made a trip over to Bimini a couple of years after I got her rigged out the way I wanted.

• • •

So, now you know how I get around to write the stories about all the great areas of Florida that fishermen and women come from all over the world trying to break records.

A bit later I'll tell you how I wound up in Chokoloskee to write a book about ghosts, but first I'll tell you a little about Chokoloskee and Everglades City.

Everglades City became the Collier County Seat in 1923 and remained that way for many years, until a hurricane devastated the little fishing village. They moved it to East Naples in 1962, and most of the old timers who have been in EC all their lives are glad they did.

Chokoloskee was one of the Ten Thousands Islands until 1956 when a causeway was put in to link it with Everglades City. Chokoloskee would never be considered mountainous terrain by the flocks of snowbuzzards who now fly in every winter, but when the storms hit, those twenty-foot-high shell mounds that the Calusa Indians created and left behind a couple thousand years ago, sure seem like mountains to the local folks who get on top of 'em till the storm passes.

A commercial fisherman that I met actually had fill brought in, and he created his own Mt. Chokoloskee to build his house on top of.

Chokoloskee Bay is ten miles long and two miles wide, and is filled with oyster bars that'll take the bottom out of a boat if the passageways aren't learned before you go flying across the bay in your new fishing speedboat. That sounds like an oxymoron t'me, because I don't get in a hurry when I'm fishing to relax. I wonder if they got the moron part of that word by watchin a guy fishing while running his speedboat back n' forth like a moron?

Once you've learned how to get around in the bay without tearing the bottom out of your boat, or at least not a second time, and you're through the pass and on out into the waters beyond the Ten Thousand Islands, you'll find some of the best fishing on this planet.

Both places became commercial fishing towns in a big way about the time WW-II ended and the boys came back home. At about the same time, an ex-soldier I knew down in Key Largo, named Ricky Wollferts, was trying to figure out what kind of traps to build that he could catch crawfish in, (Yankees call 'em lobsters, even though theirs look more like crabs, but we call ours crawfish) a guy in Chokoloskee, named Totch Brown, had just returned from the war too and began building traps to catch stone crabs. I doubt they ever met, but both men loved where they lived and lived to fish for their livelihood.

Before too long they were doing well at trapping, so naturally other men began building traps, and two new industries were born. I don't know if the Green Gestapo realize it, but they're changing lots of lives by discarding their common sense and marching to the Al Gore Boogie Woogie in hopes, I reckon, of being awarded a green star by Big Al. Maybe they'll wake up in time for the sons of the fishermen who pioneered that area to see their sons head out in the wee hours to spend the day on their commercial boat doing what they love and earn a living doing it.

• • •

Now, about all those ghosts that a lot of the people around Chokoloskee have been seeing ever since that spoiled little fella from Sebring had his men fire up his collection of Tonka Trucks and tore out Mamie Drive. After that he had a fence put up all around the property he bought, which didn't include the property that the Smallwood Trading Post and Museum sat on, but he fenced that in too, which no longer allowed the public to visit the 100 year old trading post, even though it was legally placed in the Public Domain.

That was about Easter of 2011. I don't really know if it's true, but I heard that the little guy had a real fit when he was told that he couldn't just up n' tear out the road leading to the Smallwood Trading Post, even if he did own some property on both sides of it.

I can't imagine what would motivate someone to tear out a road, which was decreed to be part of the public domain, and had been named almost a century ago, when it was a dirt road, to honor Mamie, the wife of Ted Smallwood, the man who built the Smallwood Trading Post. Well, a thought did flicker and turn on a light of wisdom inside my head. If, during those six months that the trading post was shut down due to the only access road being fenced off, it was to *accidentally* burn down, then that little fella from Sebring could step up in his elevated cowboy boots and look up at Lynn Smallwood, the granddaughter that re-opened her grandpa's trading post back in the 80s, and offer to buy the property.

A guy I've known for at least 40 years, one of the Brown boys, from a family that has been living in the area for over a century, told me that he was watching when the guy had his meltdown. "Py, that little guy was wearing a sailor suit just like I seen in them old movies, short pants, a bandanner roun his neck, and a little white sailor hat. He screamed that he could do anything with that Mamie Road he wanted to, 'cause he owned it. He flopped down on his back and began kicking them short little ole legs every which way. He finally jumped up n' ran over to one o' them big ole dozers he brung with him, and started screamin and pointin and a'tellin his men to dig up the road n' fence off the whole goldanged area."

He turned toward me and shook his head up n' down, kinda twitchy like, "Py, that's izactly what he said, "fence off the whole goldanged area." He sipped his can of warm beer, then added, "I reckon he figgered he could do whatever t'hell he wanted to roun heah, cause he kept sayin there ain't nobody livin here cept a buncha ignernt fishermen."

1

Robert the Doll

KEY WEST HAS ALWAYS HAD GHOSTS, AND THE more I researched it the more I understood why. By far the majority of ghosts that are still wandering around, where they can be seen occasionally by people with sensitive receptors in their brain are the by-product of violent actions that ended in their death.

The southernmost point of the Continental United States was in years past the home base of pirates who sailed the seas in search of fortune and adventure. They viewed life, theirs and the lives of all who crossed paths with them, as an extremely tenuous and temporary state of existence.

Men, women, and children much too young to be out on their own, were often seen wandering the streets of Key West in search of food to appease the moment's hunger. The perfect end of good day was to locate any place to sleep off their exhaustion in preparation for one more day of living.

During those days of bare existence in a seaside city in the warm latitudes, rivaled only by her sister-city, Port Royal Jamaica, finding a dead body, young or old, was of no concern to those who lived through another night of debauchery to face one more day of ribald excitement and adventure.

Is it then, any wonder that by passing from this life to the next, whatever that might be, in such a care-less manner, unconcerned by all who knew the cadaver while it still had life and hope for a future, that they refuse to move on?

Regardless the high expectations that many still hold to, in hopes of being rewarded with a puffy white cloud on which to sit and sing His praises for eternity, life itself is still broken down to a pile of energy.

Perhaps the person, who didn't make it through the night, might actually be up there somewhere singing his or her little heart out, but the energy that surged through that water-based bundle of bone, muscle, and fat, didn't have time to accomplish its mission. It had a goal, but because of foolish actions by the vessel carrying it around, it was left behind to attempt the tying together of many loose ends.

Any wonder then, that it rants and rattles in attics, and vents its frustrations in all manner of methods? Of course not. I would be so pissed off if it happened to me that you and your life would not be safe in my presence.

I first met Robert the Doll in 1951 when I made that resplendent trip to Key West. I was 16 and summer had burst open the gates of my incarceration at Miami Tech. My life-sentence had been temporarily commuted.

I was learning *readin, writin,* and *rithmatic* half the day to get my high school diploma, and since it was a tech school, I was studying journalism the second half. But I'll tell you, it was hard for me to stay in that fourteen story building during those first few weeks of summer, and when let out, off I went like a rocket. Hattie always told her friends that she kept a picture of me taped to the fridge so she wouldn't forget what I looked like.

We lived in a houseboat on the Miami River, and when Elrod (don't know why I never called him dad. I guess because everyone called him Elrod. Never called Hattie mom either. All I ever heard her called was Hattie.) bought me a boat, I was seldom home after that when the sun was still up. That 13' 4" boat had a little 2 ¼ HP Evinrude outboard motor, and I doubt there was ever a little kicker and boat that covered as much territory. Me n' whatever dog I had at the time would load up supplies and away we'd go for the weekend. I got it when I was 11 and when I went to Key West at 16 it was still tied right next to our houseboat that was docked at a Yacht Basin on the Miami River.

Hattie's friend Eloise and her husband, Garcia, were born in Cuba but came across the Gulfstream in the 20s on a fishing boat while they were still just kids, and settled in Miami with their folks. In 1951 lots of people went over to Cuba on vacation, and that's what they had planned.

Their son, Jorge, was my age and we even went to school together at Ada Merritt Elementary School in downtown Miami before they moved to Key West.

When Eloise called Hattie and told her I was welcome to come along with them, mom didn't even ask me when I got home. She knew that I'd be going with them. Eloise and Garcia were still fishing, but by then they had bought a nice big charter boat and were taking the tourists that came to Key West every winter out into the Gulfstream for some big time fishing.

Back then we hardly ever saw a snowbuzzard in our Florida during summer, so it was a good time to go on vacation. We stayed over there in Cuba a month and I loved every minute of it, because we went out fishing nearly every day. When Garcia took us all out fishing it was a great trip, but also a trip to make money to pay for everything we needed each day. He's the man that showed me how much better it is fishing with a handline instead of a rod n' reel—and that's what I still use in deeper water. We anchored all night at a place called Cay Sal down off the north coast of Cuba, not too far east of Havana. It's just a clump of rocks on a reef that has a light on it. Four of us brought more than four hundred pounds of grouper and snapper over the stern that night.

We gutted 'em all and put the whole batch of fish in the big boxes full of ice that sit on the deck waiting to be filled. Then we all snoozed a while before heading back to Matanzas. They were both born there and it's a really nice little town. Sits up at the end of a small bay and is close enough to Havana that we rode in with their friends twice to spend the day.

When we returned to Key West I called Hattie and Elrod to let 'em know that I was back. Eloise got on and told Hattie it would be fine with them if I could stay until school started, so I could spend time with Jorge. Hattie said okay, so I knew it was gonna be the best summer yet.

Garcia had already told us that he planned to go west to the Marquesas to fish the deep area along there and then anchor on the sandy areas close to that circle of keys. "If we don't do any good there," he said, "we'll go on west to the Dry Tortugas and fish there. We can anchor inside Fort Jefferson if a storm comes up."

The Marquesas Keys are 30 miles from Key West, and the Dry Tortugas where Fort Jefferson is lies about 40 miles west of there. I'd never been to either place and looked forward to the trip.

Garcia was gonna spend a couple days working on the boat, so Jorge said he'd take me to see a real voodoo doll. "My daddy has known a man named Eugene Otto for many years," Jorge said as we walked past the turtle kraals down by the waterfront. "He's an artist and writes stuff too, but I ain't really into that sorta thing." Jorge was usually a quiet kid, but I could tell that he was really excited about something, so I kept my mouth shut for a change, and just waited for him to continue as we walked along Duval Street toward where this guy lived.

"He's pretty old," Jorge finally continued, "older than my dad, anyway, but he's a real friendly guy and is also pretty interesting." He turned toward me and lifted his black eyebrows and closed his dark eyes while cocking his head a bit, "At least for an old guy."

We walked on in silence again for a couple of blocks before Jorge said anything. "He's got this voodoo doll that a servant gave him when he was still just a kid, probably a lot younger than we are now. I heard Eugene tell daddy that the servant was a voodoo priest brought here from Haiti against his will and carried a doll he named Robert with him. I asked Eugene if I could see the doll and he told me he was busy that day, but if I came back some other time a little earlier in the day, then he would let me see Robert." He looked at me really hard for a minute or so then asked, "Are you scared of things like that, Py?"

"I dunno, Eugene," I blurted out, "ain't never been around any voodoo dolls."

We walked on in silence and stayed close to each other until we finally stopped in front of a huge old house with a black iron fence around it. "Is this where the doll is?" I asked Jorge that while I leaned way back to look up at the pointed thing on the top of the house.

"Yeah, Mister Otto has a room upstairs that he had all of Robert's stuff put in, and that's where the doll is s'pose to stay, but he told daddy that lotsa people swear they've seen Robert lookin out them skinny windows on the top floor," he looked at me with raised eyes, "and that ain't where the doll stays." Jorge pointed up at the narrow windows just below what looked to me back then like the top of a fort. I later learned that it was a widow's walk.

"That's kinda spooky," I said but laughed a little when I said it. "If I ever saw Bugs Bunny or Frankenstein or The

Mummy lookin out a window at me I'd get away from that house n' never go near it again."

Jorge opened the front gate and said, "Daddy told Ma that lotsa people here in Key West won't go anywhere near this house, because of that voodoo doll, Robert."

Jorge led the way through the gate, and after closing it I followed him toward the huge wooden front door. I stayed on the stone path while he went up the five steps and pushed the doorbell. I almost yelled when that guy in the Mummy movies, who burned some leaves to wake the Mummy up, pulled a window curtain back and looked out at us. If it wasn't John Carradine then he sure coulda made money by filling in when he was sick or the director wanted him to have a twin.

He didn't just peek out at us, he stayed right there and stared at us—creepy. I was ready to get the heck outa there and forget all about Robert the Voodoo Doll—when the door opened. The Mummy's ghoul smiled and said, "Jorge, am I correct?"

The ghoul actually smiled when Jorge nodded and said, "Yessir."

"Mister Otto said he was expecting you one day this week." He looked past Jorge at me and I got goosebumps, "I see you've brought a friend."

Probably needs some fresh new blood for the Mummy, I thought.

He stepped back and opened the door farther so we had room to enter the hallway. He was Mister Otto's houseman and chauffer, and actually seemed like a very pleasant old guy, but it took me a while to get over the shock of seeing the Mummy's ghoul look out at me like that. Especially since me n' Jorge were going into a house where a Voodoo Doll wandered around at all hours of the night.

"Mister Otto had Missus Hathaway fry up those nice yellowtail snappers that your father brought us last week when you n' him stopped by. Tell Garcia that we all enjoyed them very much."

"I thought I heard voices," Mister Otto said with a smile as he opened a door along the hall and looked out.

"I was just telling Jorge and his friend how much we all enjoyed those fresh yellowtail snappers that Garcia gave us."

"Hello Jorge, and who do we have here?"

"He's my friend Py, from Miami. He's gonna be a writer like you."

"Hello, Py." He took a step forward and held his hand out, which I shook. "Writing can be a very lonesome endeavor and requires a great deal of self-discipline." He had a very pleasant smile as he shook my hand. Letting go he turned to Jorge, "Have you come to see Robert?"

"Yessir, I been telling Py all about him, and he'd like to see him too, if you don't mind."

"Why certainly he can accompany you to see Robert. I still have quite a bit to do, so I'll get back to it. Mister Gladwell will guide you both to Robert's room." He smiled again, but then furrowed his eyebrows and a slight frown crossed his wrinkled face, "Do be careful, boys, because he has been a bit mischievous lately. Those Haitians that live over on Elizabeth Street made a paper doll that looked like Robert and hung it from the streetlight outside where he could see it, and then set it afire."

Mister *Carradine* led the way up the stairs to the second story, with us as close to him as possible. He dug a huge skeleton key out of his pocket, and after shoving it into the hole on the door to Robert's room, he turned and looked real serious when he spoke. "We keep his door locked, but somehow Robert manages to go up to the top floor at times so he can look out the windows." He then turned the key and shoved the door open.

Once we were inside, the old man nodded toward the far wall. Against the wall was a really neat table with ball and claw legs, and all stained a dark shiny color that looked like it might have fifty layers of varnish on it, *or maybe its blood*, I thought. It sat by itself right in the center of the wall.

I stood beside Jorge and watched as Mister Gladwell... (I am not going to call him anything else for a while, because he really did appear to be a nice old man—BUT as you will see later in this story, appearances can be deceiving. Reasons will surface why I once again reverted to calling him the Mummy's Ghoul)...walked to the wall where a small white rope ran from the top of what looked like a big version of a cloth cover used to go down over a parrot's cage to keep them from singing and mumbling all night.

He unwrapped the rope from a cleat screwed into the darkly varnished wooden wall behind the table and slowly raised the cover. I never did ask Jorge what he felt at that very moment, but when I looked at Robert for the very first time, a chill rushed through me like nothing I had ever experienced, and I don't mind telling the entire world that it's happened every time I've looked at him since that day. That was over half a century ago, and I've looked into those death-eyes about a dozen times since then while living in Key West. I still get the same chill, and it's as if my blood is about to freeze—'creepy little dwarf' doesn't even come close to describing that wicked little voodoo death doll.

After securing the rope back onto the wall cleat, Mister Gladwell handed Jorge the key and said to be sure to lock the door after we were finished. He had work downstairs to do and asked that we bring him the key. "Take your time, boys," a big smile crossed his spooky old face and I thought at the time that it was an odd smile—sorta crooked and twisted.

Jorge stood there silently looking at Robert for about a minute, but then turned away saying, "Just another doll as far as I can see." He looked at me then, "You see some voodoo stuff in it, Py?"

I was sorta mesmerized that first time I guess, and he turned away when I didn't answer him. He said he was going to see if he could find the stairs up to the next floor, and he would be back down in a minute if he did. And then, he said, "We can go up and look out those skinny windows and see what Robert the Doll was lookin at." He grinned and held both arms straight up as he groaned, "I am the devil doll." He laughed and ran off to see what was up there.

I turned back and couldn't take my eyes off of Robert, so I just sorta mumbled something, and heard Jorge run down the hall. I started to say, don't close the door, but I heard it shut, so I automatically looked at it. When I turned back to Robert, the skin around his eyes had wrinkled and he was leaning forward a little, or at least it seemed to me that he was. *It was*, I thought at the time, *as if he wanted to get a better look at me.*

After about a minute I realized that I had been holding my breath, so I slowly exhaled, and then took a very deep breath, and that's when it happened.

I was looking straight into Robert's eyes when his odd head bent over to the left—his left, not mine...maybe it's left? . . . whatever!

I was holding my breath again when his mouth opened. It didn't open much, but enough for me to see a small tongue wriggling around in there like a fishing worm trying not to let a finger and thumb grab it.

I wasn't a scardy-cat kid, or a teenager afraid of his own shadow. Anyone who has known me as an adult for many years will certainly say that I'm not easily spooked, or that I'll walk around the block before walking under a ladder, or freak out if a black cat crosses my path, or fall victim to that sorta thing—because I don't. But this doll was another matter.

I noticed that there was dust on the table around Robert the Doll. The rest of the table seemed to shine, so I pulled my finger across it. Sure enough, there wasn't even a hint of dust on my finger. I had noticed an odd smell when I walked to the table, so I smelled the finger I had rubbed across the table—nothing, no odor at all, but I could still smell that damp odor. Not a mildew odor like my clothes got when I tossed 'em into the drawer under my bunk on our houseboat. This odor was different from any I had ever smelled.

I don't know why I did it, but without even thinking about it I walked around the corner of the table and leaned toward the doll. Pulling my finger through the dust—or whatever it was, I then lifted it to my nose and sniffed. It was so pungent I almost gagged. *That's what The Mummy would smell like,* was my first thought. I started to reach out and scoop up some of that dust on the side of my hand—until I saw Robert the Doll move.

When I saw that wormy little tongue inside Robert the Doll's mouth moving, and his squinted eyes looking into mine as he leaned even farther forward, to close the gap between our minds I suppose—I took off.

If that door had locked for whatever reason, when Jorge had closed it behind him, major repairs would have been required. I doubt that a second attempt to get it to open, if it hadn't on my first try, would have seemed logical at that moment—but I probably wouldn't have tried, and gone right through it.

I closed the door, and just about the time my breath had returned to its normal cadence, Jorge came down the stairs and stepped into the hallway. "The door at the top o' these stairs," he said, "was unlocked, but the one to that next room up and the other door to that widow's walk were both locked." His pointed chin motioned toward Robert's door, "Finished in there?"

"Yeah," I answered softly to mask my fright, "ain't much t'see, just another doll. Might as well lock up and head back to the boat n' see if your dad needs help."

...

In 1955 I jumped at the opportunity to go to Key West with the magazine's senior writer. The guy was doing a special edition article on a very popular author that had a home there. Ernest Hemingway was bringing in some really nice billfish regularly, so the Key West Chamber of Commerce made a deal with the magazine to pay the expenses to have their head writer spend two days there fishing with Hemingway.

He said, "Py, you have friends down there to stay at, so you're welcome to ride along if you want."

I thanked Louie, that was his name, Louie Powell, and he would become a well-known writer a few years later. He was on his way to the top when he let the magazine editor talk him into strapping himself to a guy that was getting a lot of publicity by jumping out of airplanes and doing a bit of maneuvering before opening his parachute. They both died on the very first attempt to make a jump strapped together.

~ A FEW YEARS LATER ~

It was November and quite a few tourists were in Key West to do some deep sea fishing. Garcia was booked solid through March. Jorge was working on the boat and he was making good money. Garcia said there wouldn't be room for me to fish, but if I wasn't doing anything, I could ride along, so I jumped aboard.

The second day out, a woman got so seasick that the guy she was with finally asked Garcia to head in early. Once we were docked I told Jorge, who had to clean up the boat, that I wanted to look up a friend, and I'd be home a little later. "Take my bicycle," he said pointing at a new one chained to a lamp post, "and I'll ride with pop." He tossed me the key and a minute later I was pedaling toward Mister Otto's house.

After chaining the bike to his wrought-iron fence I went up the steps and rang the bell. I kept glancing at the side window that Mister Gladwell had peered out at us from during that first visit, but he never showed. Finally the door opened, and I almost screamed, because there he stood looking down at me—but he'd changed. I couldn't quite put my finger on it, but something about him had changed. He was *different*.

"Nice to see you again, Mister Lam, do come in." I couldn't believe he remembered my last name. *Maybe he has me marked as a blood donor for his mummy?* I followed him along the hall until he stopped, and while opening a door, motioned for me to enter the small room. "Please have a seat and I'll tell Mister Otto that you are here."

I entered what had at some point in the far distant past been a small sitting room. It was very tastefully furnished and the walls were covered with tapestries that looked old enough to have come from a Persian King's home. I sat at a small lacquered table beside a large permanent window overlooking similar houses, all crammed much too close together. I caught a glimpse of the sea between them and spotted a huge shrimp boat with her booms out. *She's too close to shore to be dragging nets,* I thought as I watched. *Bet she's rigged out to go snapper fishing over near Campeche Mexico, and those are flopper-stoppers at the end of the booms to make her roll a bit less so they'll have a smoother trip.*

I thought about the change in Mister Gladwell. *He sure has aged a lot in five years.* But that's not what I noticed. *He's still as ghoulish looking as he was, but now he has an evil sorta look, like he might actually be able to burn some tano leaves, or whatever the heck kind of leaves those were that ole John Carradine was burning to wake up The Mummy.*

I think I actually jumped a little when he stepped into the room and said, "Mister Otto would like to know if you care to have tea with him in ten minutes."

"Yes," I said before realizing that Mister Gladwell would make it, "thank you very much." *I sure hope it's not made with those mummy-waking tano leaves.*

"Very good sir, he'll be right here to join you as soon as he completes a letter."

I watched as he slowly turned and headed toward the rear of the house, probably the kitchen. *John made some tea in a Mummy movie once and it turned the guy who was looking for The Mummy into a zombie.* I looked out the window but couldn't see the shrimper. *I ain't drinkin no darn tea made by The Mummy's ghoul.* I took a deep breath and let it out slowly to get my brain working again. *You're acting like some kinda frightened darn Girl Scout, Py, getcher act together.* At that moment Mister Otto said "Hello again, Py," and entered the room, followed by Mister Gladwell carrying a silver tea service.

During tea I asked if he would mind if I had another look at Robert.

"Of course not, Py, but I'm somewhat curious why, when so many people go out of their way to not get near this house after they've learned about Robert the Doll."

He sipped his tea and looked at me over the rim. "I've never forgotten that first time, Mister Otto, and I've been thinking about writing something, maybe even a book, about voodoo dolls, spirits of pirates, ghosts, and a bunch of other things like that." I smiled at him and added, "I've been hearing a lot lately from people who have lived here in Key West a long time. They talk about ghosts, and also voodoo, zombies, restless spirits, and som'n I heard about called Santeria." After I said that, I noticed that Mister Gladwell was looking at me with a twisted, and very cruel expression—his eyelids actually pinched together as slits.

"Well, Py, I've read a few of your articles about fishing in the waters around these Keys and both coasts, and found them very interesting. If you decide to write a book about ghosts and strange entities like Robert, I'm quite certain that it'll be a good read and well received."

"I would like very much to read it too, Mister Lam."

I turned toward Mister Gladwell expecting him to have a sarcastic smile on his crooked face. He looked at me with a very serious face and said, "Especially if you write a chapter about Robert."

I was somewhat surprised but didn't let it show, and smiled when I replied, "I'll see to it that you gentlemen get the first two copies off the press."

"Thank you, Py," Mister Otto said, "and we'll promote it to all of our friends."

After finishing our tea, Mister Gladwell placed the china on a silver tray and said he'd be right back to escort me up to Robert the Doll's room.

Moments later I was following him up the stairs toward Robert's room, but an uneasy feeling had found a home among the short hairs on my neck—they were all standing up. At the door he fumbled with his keys until he located the correct one, and then inserted a huge old skeleton key into the hole. I was surprised how many times he turned that big ole key until there was a loud kinda click, and the door opened a crack.

He pulled the heavy, solid oak door open and removed the key. With an expressionless, stone-like face he said, "Enjoy your visit with Robert, Mister Lam, and do not forget," he paused as he removed the skeleton key from his ring, "to lock it when you leave." He handed me the key, and without a word he turned and headed up the stairs leading to the upper story.

When I heard a key being inserted into the keyhole and turned, I puzzled over why he would lock that door behind him. When I heard his huge shoes clunking up the wooden stair treads, I closed Robert the Doll's door. Before I approached the darkly stained table where he sat under his parrot-hood, I turned and looked at the closed door. I walked over and opened it, and then after shoving it back against the wall, I looked in both directions for something that would keep it there.

Finding nothing that would work, and feeling a bit silly because the door stayed where I placed it, I re-entered the room and went straight to the rope that was wrapped around a cleat. It was brass and looked like it mighta spent many years on a sailing vessel. The screws holding it to the pickwick pine boards were also made of brass and so buggered up that I figured they had probably held the cleat to a gunwale or mast on a ship.

While standing there alone I looked around the room. *Everything is exactly as it was when Jorge and I came here to see Robert.* I thought it was odd, because nothing was ever in the same place when I lived on the houseboat with Hattie and Elrod. *Ah well, everyone's got their own ideas how things oughta be.*

After loosening the two half hitches, I unwrapped the rest of the small nylon rope and slowly raised the parrot-hood. I didn't realize that I was holding my breath again as the hood raised. First revealed were his nubby little shoes, and then his outstretched legs. Before continuing to raise the hood, I let my breath flow out in a loud whoosh.

I almost let go of the rope when I noticed that Robert's head was moving. Very slowly but it was moving, and by the time I had the rope tied back on the cleat, he...it, I guess *it* is what the doll oughta be called, because *he* makes the thing seem human. I still to this day don't know what it is, but it darn sure ain't human.

Anyway, it had rotated its head forty-five degrees in the time it took me to secure the rope. It was looking straight ahead when I began raising that hood. After tossing a pair of half-hitches on the cleat, I almost yelped like a puppy when I looked up.

As I stood watching, I noticed that his strange doll-like little mouth was twisting into something that I suppose could be considered a smile, and Robert the Doll was looking straight into my eyes. Spooky doesn't even come close to explaining how I felt at that moment.

I moved quickly from the cleat on the wall and rounded the end of the table. I didn't stop or look at anything until I was at the end of the long oak table. When I finally took a look in the doll's direction, I swallowed and stepped back.

I still have a difficult time accepting the events of that short time I spent alone with Robert the Doll that day, but I know they're all true. After regaining my composure I stepped close to the table and went down to my knees. I leaned in and looked for wires, steel rods, and anything else that a person could remotely control movement of the doll. There was not a sign of anything that would explain what I had just seen, but I scooted in on my knees just a bit farther and looked the area beneath Robert over very, very thoroughly—still nothing.

I crabbed back out and stood up. Robert was holding his stuffed toy lion and looking straight out into the room, instead of staring at me like before. I was just beginning to think that maybe I had imagined all of it when his head moved slowly until his beady, red little eyes were locked to mine again.

I was so shocked by those evil little eyes that I froze where I stood for a moment. *My God,* I thought, *Robert the Doll is really alive.* My mind began racing, and I twisted my wrist to look at my watch. *I've been in here less than ten minutes and it seems more like an hour.*

I was still looking into the doll's eyes when its lips began moving.

You can die.

The voice was so scratchy and hoarse that I wheeled around so fast I very nearly fell. *You can die,* it said again. I froze in place momentarily, but then slowly turned toward Robert. His eyes (I was already referring to Robert as *he* again) were no longer dull little spots sunken back into his head. They glowed red, way back in the sockets as though light was coming from a deep tunnel. It was a wet light and had a milky red glow to it, and my first thought was, *it looks as if light is radiating through blood.*

I almost lunged at the cleat where the hood rope was secured. As fast as my hands and fingers would work I got the rope off the cleat and let it slide through my hands. A second later the hood was resting on the table, so I tied it off again and turned to leave.

You can die. That same scratchy voice.

I paused in the doorway before stepping into the hall. *You can die.* The hood had a hard ring on the bottom, probably steel, to keep it in place. I had left a little slack in the rope before I tied it off, but as I stood in the doorway that hood was not resting against the table—it was moving. I swear it was as if Robert was kicking it.

I pulled the door away from the wall and started to close it when that scratchy voice said again, *you can die.*

Later that same day, I went with Jorge to a very small restaurant just down the street, a short walk from the turtle kraals. It was around the corner from where his dad's boat was docked.

The owner was an older Cuban lady that came to Key West with her parents about seventy years earlier. "Pop's known Maggie forever," Jorge turned toward me, "her real name is Magdalena, but everybody calls her Maggie." His infectious grin warmed me, "Pop used to work on her husband, Arturo's, boat when he was still alive. Even though my dad had his own boat, he went out with Arturo often to learn how that old man brought in a lot more yellow-tail and yellow-eye snappers than anyone. The tourists pay more for those two if they're freshly caught. "

After a sip of iced tea, Jorge put his glass back down on the napkin and shook his head, "Boy oh boy, Py, pop n' Arturo brought in some big catches. Pop told me they once anchored on the reef one night not very far from the lighthouse, and chummed up a school of yellow-tail that stayed right there a few hands from the stern until they ran out of chum. They came in at dawn and put over six hundred pounds on the dock." He turned back shaking his head again, "Imagine an old guy and pop, who was still just a kid, and really didn't know a whole lot about commercial fishing, putting that many fish in chill barrels with just handlines."

"Boy," I said, "no wonder he kept going out with the guy on his boat."

"Yeah, he learned a lot from ole Arturo."

The guy writing the article about Hemingway fishing near Key West came by to tell me we would head back to Miami at noon the next day. When Jorge's dad asked if I'd like to attend church with them later that night I said yes. I'm not a religious man but I like to learn about the habits and many other things that the different ethnic groups are emotionally involved in.

Growing up in the Miami area, that began evolving into a Mecca for Hispanic, Haitian, and many other ethnic groups in the 80s, I immediately recognized the signs of Santeria as the religion being observed by the people in the small one room building we entered.

"Are you familiar at all with our Santeria religion, Py?" Garcia whispered.

"Yes," I answered quietly, "it's very popular among the Cuban families that I'm acquainted with."

"Is this the first time you've been to a Santeria service, Py?" Eloise spoke in such a soft whisper that I missed a few words, but understood what she was saying.

"Yes," I whispered back, "it is."

She shook her head up and down, "It was our religion when we lived in Cuba." She looked a little self-righteous when she said, "It is a religion that is very good for the common people."

I nodded as though I agreed, but almost stumbled as I followed the family toward the back of the room where I could see the altar. I silently gasped when I saw who was standing next to it. It was Mister Gladwell, and he was talking to a huge, fat, black man. The fat man was dressed in a shiny black silk suit, and his frayed black tie hung in front of an almost white shirt like a small dead animal. The coat was also showing large wet areas around his armpits.

I heard a small bell ring and watched as all the people that were outside began streaming in. It was a little bit unsettling when the wide door was closed and locked, but not as much as when I saw the two largest men among the group take a position in front of the door with muscular arms across their huge chest. They were obviously there to prevent outsiders in or insiders out—the latter was disturbing.

I wasn't surprised when the fat black man stepped up on a portable podium that was carried out from a back room.

Thirty minutes later I was still wishing I had taken the Spanish language course that was offered at Miami Tech. I had been watching Mister Gladwell while the guest priest (Eloise had whispered that info to me) was rattling off a message to his flock. It all sounded like a hen-house opera to me, so while facing forward toward the priest I rotated my eyes to the corner of my glasses.

I'd done it a few times, and each time, Mister Gladwell was intently listening to the priest. For that reason I was a bit more than just surprised when he stood, and looked at me with that same dead-pan evil stare for a moment.

Eloise continued looking straight at the black man up at the podium, but leaned close to whisper in my ear, "He is a Santeria priest and a very good friend of our own priest, Father Emmanuel." Fats had quite obviously just introduced The Mummy's Ghoul by the way everyone stopped their whispering, which they'd been doing like snakes at a hiss convention.

He exchanged places with Fats, and stood there on the podium in that silent room for a long moment as his eyes slowly roamed across everyone, including me. But when he stopped, and stared at me again through nearly closed slits, I got very uncomfortable.

When he began speaking to his audience in Spanish I had a difficult time believing it was the same man that I had followed up the stairs earlier that same day. His Spanish flowed out so fast and smooth that I started wondering if his real name was Gladwell.

Later that night Eloise told me that his real name was Vladimir Polenka, and he was at one time the bodyguard to Fulgencio Batista, the President of Cuba.

"He was a very powerful man in Cuba until a couple of years ago." She pinched her lips and shook her head back and forth, "He got involved with the Voodoo aspects of our religion and lost his job as head of Presidential Security, a very good position in Cuba."

Eloise paused a moment before adding, "He was born in Russia but his parents moved to Cuba when he was very young. He got out of Cuba alive only because of his many Russian friends. They took him by boat out to a big commercial lobster vessel that was returning to Key West from Cochinas Bank. He's been here ever since, working as Mister Otto's butler, chauffeur, and also all-around handyman. Having no papers showing that he is here legally is a big and possibly costly problem if INS hears about him." She took a long hard look at me, unusual for her, and then said, "Py, please don't write or say anything about him, because he has helped us a lot in the creation of our new church here in Key West."

I smiled and assured her that I would do nothing that would jeopardize his position in Key West. Inside though, I thought, *he's probably gonna make zombies or mummies of everyone in this church.*

The newspaper guy was right on time the following day. It was a pleasant hundred mile drive back up the Keys to Key Largo, where we stopped at the Pilot House Bar & Grill. We each had a fried grouper sandwich, fresh-cut french-fries, and a cold draft beer for him and a glass of real iced tea for me, which was so dark I could barely see the spoon I used to stir the sugar.

The owner's name was Moon Mullins, which he got, or so the columnist said, from a cartoon strip character that he resembled.

Louie Powell had met Moon a few years earlier at a place up on the highway named The Rod and Reel. They had a couple of beers while talking about the groupers that Moon regularly caught out at a place near the reef called The Elbow. Louie made arrangements to go with him one evening, and later he talked the magazine into paying all expenses. I read the piece and had to admit that it was good—good pictures too.

Louie said he'd been coming here ever since he went to work for the magazine. He'd probably worked a deal to get the magazine to pay all the expenses for him to go fishing, and then he'd write an article about it. That trip to Key West with Louie is what got me thinking about doing the same thing.

About a week after that trip to Key West I was sipping coffee and reading the Miami Herald when I saw an article with a very unusual heading: Key West VOODOO PRIEST KILLED.

I sipped my hot coffee and began reading, but almost choked when I got to the third line...*Robert the Doll's owner, Mister Otto...*

I had to read it again to be sure. *Wow!* I thought, and continued reading...

> *...realized that the doll was gone when he went upstairs and saw the door to the room where he kept the doll, standing open. "Robert is a very valuable doll," he later told this reporter, "and when Mister Gladwell was nowhere to be seen, I felt certain that it was him that took Robert."*

I finished the entire article, and then read it again to be sure I hadn't read something into it that wasn't there—it was that crazy.

> *Vladimir Polenka was a very disturbed man. According to Mister Otto, Vladimir came to him a week earlier and asked him to give Robert to him so he could crucify the doll and save all of the common people in Cuba. He explained to Mister*

Otto that a curse was placed on all Cubans by the doll's first owner. A Cuban ex-prisoner in Haiti had made Robert while in prison and then hexed all Cubans by placing a curse on the doll. Vladimir Polenka researched it all while living in Cuba, and then changed his name to Mister Boris Gladwell. He secured a position in Key West with the doll's new owner, Eugene Otto. By using false documents, he was able to stay close to the doll until he could arrange the crucifixion. He had been a Santeria Priest in Cuba, so it was easy to start a new church in Key West.

The article went on to explain that Mister Otto knew the location of Mister Gladwell's church, because the small building was owned by a friend. He called the police first, and then hired a taxi to take him there. Arriving before the police might easily have cost him his life, because when he first walked into the house, Vladimir was preparing Robert the Doll for crucifixion.

When he turned and spotted Mister Otto, Vladimir was chanting in a strange foreign tongue, but immediately stopped. He pulled a huge machete from a leather sheath attached to his belt and ran screaming toward Mister Otto, with the big knife held high and ready for a decapitating blow.

The well-timed and fortuitous arrival of that one lone police officer ended Vladimir's contrived execution of both Robert the Doll and its owner, Mister Otto. At the moment a pair of 9 mm slugs from the officer's pistol entered Vladimir's brain from only several feet away, Mister Otto was standing frozen in place and terrified, with both eyes riveted to the razor sharp machete. He later told a reporter that he now understood why a deer freezes in the lights of an automobile.

Robert the Doll was returned to Mister Otto early on the following day after the crime scene investigators had photographed everything, including, to the chagrin of the old Cuban who was the official police photographer, Robert the Doll. As a member of Vladimir's Santeria Church, the old man tried to convince the Captain that it would serve no purpose to photograph the doll.

~ OOO ~

Robert Eugene Otto was the doll's owner until 1974 when he died...a new family bought their house, and a 10 year old girl became the dolls owner. She still claims that the doll once tried to kill her, "And he moves around on his own all the time," she told a reporter.

Robert is now on display at the Fort East Martello Museum until October when he is rotated to the Old Post Office and Customhouse in downtown Key West. He is watched by an armed guard 24/7.

A word of warning to all who decide to visit Robert the Doll during a Key West vacation. Prior to visiting this evil entity, have your crucifix blessed, wear a fresh garlic bulb around your neck, get a pistol and have it filled with silver bullets, and then update your last will and testament. Do not lock eyes with this harmless looking doll, or all of your remaining dreams might be turned into nightmares. As many have learned, Robert is anything but harmless.

2

Swamp Assignment

I RECEIVED A PHONE CALL FROM THE EDITOR OF the magazine in April 2011. I had retired eleven years earlier when I was eligible for Social Security. His father, who held the same position since he created the magazine in the early 50s, had also retired shortly after I left. So his son jumped from the senior columnist to Editor-in-Chief.

"Hello Py, how's everything in Key West?"

"Jimmy," I answered, "if I was doing any better, the Fed's would be investigating me to find out why." When I retired, home was aboard Floating Homestead, the same aluminum boat that I had lived, worked, and traveled aboard for over half a century.

"Still on a mooring, or have you moved to the dock?"

"Wouldn't move to the dock even if they offered me a free slip, electric, water, cable TV, and Internet, Jimmy."

"Yeah, I understand Py, gotta be nice n' quiet out there on a buoy. I keep telling you that I'm gonna come down n' be a pain in the ass guest one of these days, and I will, but it has been really busy lately."

"Jimmy, you weren't a pain when you were a kid, and I have always enjoyed having you along when we cruised the coast together. Just c'mon down when you can." I knew he didn't call just to shoot the breeze, so I paused a moment before speaking. "Okay Jimmy, what's on your mind?"

"I'm that easy to read, huh?"

"Eeeeeyup, always was."

"Wanna get paid for writing a story about a bunch of ghosts raising hell over in Chokoloskee?"

~ OOO ~

So, as of Friday June 10th 2011, I was working again. To keep from screwing up my pension, Jimmy sent me a credit card and told me to put everything on it until I finished the story, and then toss it in with the manuscript and mail it all to him.

I'd once traveled up to Apalachicola to write about the oystermen, and another time to Ft. Pierce for an article about a couple of guys who were trying sword fishing with long lines out in the Gulfstream. Any time I traveled to get a good story, Jimmy's dad always gave me a credit card for expenses, and later handed me a nice wad of money—cash, no feds involved. I was feeling pretty darn good heading up the coast to get a story, after being idle so long and also because I was getting paid to go on a nice vacation.

I could have run across the bay towards Chokoloskee, but a wide stretch of water like that can turn mean in a heartbeat. I set the Lister at 1100 RPMs once I was in the channel heading up the bay side of the Keys.

I anchored in the shallows just beyond Marathon, and put a pot of water on the stove to boil. I cleaned two Jack Crevalle I caught trolling during a stretch where the auto-pilot did the steering.

An hour after anchoring I was eating fresh jack salad that no canned tuna salad could compete with.

A few days later I was following the coastline north, and would soon be in the shallows west of Flamingo campground in the Everglades National Park. The sky was still clear and the wind was blowing about fifteen knots from the south. It was strong enough to blow most of the mosquitos back into the swamp, so even though it was still an hour from dark, I anchored just off the mouth of Shark River. Once my plow anchor had buried in, I got out my spinning outfit and a small plastic box where I kept my favorite snook lures. I tried a spoon first, but after twenty casts that didn't excite anything out there in the water watching, I switched to a white rubber worm with red stripes. Still, not a thing out there showed the slightest interest after quite a few casts. I had a brand new Yo-Zuri lure, the small one, so I got a white rubber worm and put it on. I always count the casts when nothing's happening, and on number six, kapow, a hit.

I had been thinking about a nice fish stew all day, and knew that I had bought everything needed to make one if I could land a snook, a trout, or a redfish. I was careful not to get too anxious and try to bring whatever was on up to the surface next to the boat too soon. So I cranked in the line a bit slow to let the fish wear itself out a little. I knew there was always a hungry gang of bull sharks around the mouth of Shark River, so I was a bit anxious as my catch got closer to the boat.

I always have my long-handle dip net nearby when I'm fishing from the deck. When I spotted the head of a snook, just beneath the surface of that murky water, that I figured was at least six pounds, I grabbed the net. I had tired him enough, just enough as it turned out, because barely a moment after he slid into the net and I lifted it up, a bull at least six feet long cruised right by, just beneath the net.

The sun was just beginning to slide down into the water out on the western horizon when the fish stew gently bubbled to a finish. The head had worked its way to the surface and that big snook eye was staring up at me.

Looking at it, I recalled something that Roosevelt Cooper, the mayor of Grand Cay, Bahamas, told me when I spent a weekend on his boat writing an article about bonefishing in the Bahamas: 'No head in de pot mon, ain no fish stew wurt eatin.'

After filling up a large bowl, with the head resting atop everything, I went to the fridge and got 2 Key limes, Texas Pete, and the limeade I'd made earlier. I'm not one to forego a second helping of something so delicious, especially at the advanced age of 76. That's why I left the second lime and the bottle of Texas Pete on the counter.

By the wonderful smell that had been coming from the pot as it simmered, I knew one bowl wasn't gonna cut it. After squeezing the lime into the bowl, I gave it five dashes of ole Tex. I had already attached the swing-away food tray to the captain's chair, so I carried the bowl to it and climbed up into the chair. After plucking out the crunchy eye that had been following my every move, I turned the head over while chewing it, and repeated the process with the second eye. Mmmm, boy. *You're right, Rose, no head no stew.*

After putting everything away I opened the hatch, and then stepped out onto the roof. I keep a folding chair strapped to the railing around the propane bottles, so after assuring m'self that the mosquitos were staying in the swamp to the north of me, I opened it. A tether keeps it on the roof if I'm suddenly forced off, like I once was a couple of years earlier.

While I was sitting up there, on that long-ago day, watching the sun go down, I had no idea what the roaring noise coming out of the swamp beyond Chatham Bend was. I was anchored about a quarter mile out from the site where Mister Edgar Watson's house had sat until those government morons went and burned the darn thing to the ground—I never have figured that one out. The government can spend a fortune in grants to accumulate worthless data that will never be used. Such as 'how some birds can mate in flight, and some can't,' but they couldn't justify restoring and guarding a piece of history like

Mister Watson's homestead. Maybe that's actually where the phrase oxymoron originated—not enough oxygen for the moron's to think.

I leaned forward and gripped the rail, so I could lift up my old carcass and get outa that webbed chair. I stood there for a moment listening as the roaring grew louder. Suddenly, as though a bolt of electricity had hit me, I knew what it was.

As soon as I had that exit hatch down and latched, it was like something out of a good Dean Koonts novel. (now there's a real oxymoron, because all of his novels are good) Mosquitos so thick that they blocked out what light remained before the sun dropped into the sea swarmed over the boat. Even though all of the portholes were closed and latched, I could still hear that high-pitched hum. It sounded like an airboat so close it was gonna hit my boat.

I glanced at my watch and the big hand was sitting on top of the number 1. When the noise ceased, and what light remained could once again be seen through the front window of the wheelhouse, I looked at my watch. The big hand was now just beyond the number 5.

Twenty full minutes, I remembered thinking, *for them to move on by the boat. Musta been billions of 'em—maybe even trillions. No wonder people and animals die if they can't bury up in mud and breathe through a handkerchief or som'n till they pass by.*

Later I was lying in my bunk thinking about all of the pioneers that had passed this way with little knowledge about mosquitos and how to keep 'em from eating you or driving you crazy. I read a little more of Randy Wayne White's latest novel before dropping off to sleep.

It was pitch black when I suddenly awoke in a cold sweat and frantically bolted upright and breathing hard. My old heart was pounding like a jackhammer. A moment later I recalled the dream, more aptly described as a nightmare. Before the dream was ironed out in my still sleep-addled mind, I saw two red glowing eyes looking at me from the hallway that ran between my bunk room and the galley.

I was still trying to shake the sleep from my cobweb-filled brain when Robert the Doll's voice rocketed through my mind.

You can die.

I remained in the bunk while staring at those two hideous red circles. My mind was trying to convince me that it was a dream, but a chill ran through me that made my entire body shake. It was all I could do to pull my eyes away long enough to glance at the illuminated hands on my battery-operated wall clock. *Fifteen after midnight.* My mind was still intent on convincing my body that it was just a dream, when that spooky voice erupted again.

You can die, you can die, you can die. Heh, heh, heh, heh, gheh, gheh, gheh, grrrrrrrrrrrrrrrrrrrr.

That freaky laugh and then the growl was enough to send another chill through me. I leaned back and felt between the aluminum wall and my single mattress for the flashlight. Just as I had it in my hand with my finger searching for the rubberized on/off button, that squeaky freaky doll-voice roared loudly through my brain again.

Heh, heh, heh, heh, yes Py, you can die.

I finally got myself straightened back up, so I let my feet ease off the bed. I was watching those two red eyes when they suddenly moved slowly toward me as my feet touched the floor. I was still holding my breath as I pushed the button.

I don't know how I kept from screaming, because right there in front of me, not a foot away from the flashlight, was Robert the Doll, suspended in midair.

His red eyes began flickering as they glowed brighter. That squiggly little mouth I remembered from Key West was now a gaping tiger-like mouth full of pointed teeth. Through the fangs, which is what they really looked like, came a growl that would have stopped The Mummy in his tracks, and caused Wolfman to look for an exit. **Aarrrrggggggrrrrrrrrrrrrrrrrrrrrrrrr, you can die.**

I literally didn't know whether to shit or go blind, so I did both. I flipped off the light and dampened my shorts. Still on my feet, I flipped the flashlight back on. While watching Robert drift out through the side of the hull, I reached up and turned on the rack of LED battery operated lights overhead in the passageway.

I knew I would never get back to sleep, so I put together a fresh pot of coffee. After the fire was on under the pot I moved over slightly to get a cup from one of the recessed holders in the cabinet above the small counter. After closing the cabinet door I went to put the cup on the counter, but froze halfway down. On the counter was a thin layer of dust—or something. My stomach did a flip when I ran two fingers through whatever that was on the counter beneath my still-raised cup.

Even before sniffing my fingers I had a gut-feeling I already knew what it was. I wiped my fingers on the wash cloth before placing the cup in the sink—I didn't want it anywhere near that dust.

On shaky legs, I backed into my narrow stateroom and leaned back against the mattress. *Holy crap,* I thought, *that was no dream.* I took a deep breath before saying quietly aloud, "Robert the Doll was actually here on this boat with me."

I was still leaning against my bunk when the pot began perking. I leaned forward and then took a step closer to turn down the flame. *Darnnit,* I thought, *I hope I'm still just dreaming.*

With a full cup of coffee I headed toward my captain's chair. Once settled into it, I sipped coffee while looking at the stars. It was a beautiful calm night and the boat was barely rocking, so after sipping half the coffee my eyes began closing. I abruptly sat up and looked around. Placing the half-filled cup in the holder, I closed my sleep-filled eyes. Before dozing off, my last thoughts were, *my bet is that in the morning there'll be no coffee or cup beside me and none in the pot.* Linking my fingers together across my ample belly, I closed my eyes. *And there'll be no mummy dust on that counter.*

The sun was just beginning to dust away the shadows when my eyes fluttered open. "Nuts," I said loudly as I looked at the half-filled coffee cup."

I went to the galley and set the cup in the sink while I wiped up the mummy dust. After tossing the wad of Brawny towels into the trash can I poured the coffee from the cup into the pot after removing the grounds holder. I washed the small cup and replaced it with my huge, 'gitcherbutt movin' cup—that's why I paid six bucks for the cup at a dealer on Mallory Square in Key West. The words were fired right into the cup.

With my Paul Bunyan size cup of coffee I climbed into the chair again. As I sipped, my mind kept wandered back to those first meetings with Robert the Doll. *What in the heck did I say or do to make that little voodoo creature wanna kill me?* I began recalling all of the times I saw Robert, but nothing stood out that would have caused the doll to consider me an enemy. *Maybe Robert was reading my mind when I badmouthed his caretaker?*

Just as I polished off the last of the coffee, I recalled an event that happened during a visit to the Fort East Martello Towers in Key West on Roosevelt Blvd, where Robert is on display. One of my yachting friends was visiting aboard his yacht for Christmas just last year. He and his guests were listening with rapt attention as I told them what I knew about Robert the Doll.

One of the ladies asked, "Is it really a voodoo doll?"

"Well," I said, "it more resembles something that was pulled out of a dumpster, patched up, and dressed in a sailor suit." My smile was certainly a tongue-in-cheek effort to prevent her from carrying unfounded rumors home to Philadelphia. "What many Haitians and other island people consider an object of voodoo, I label as a good hoaxster's efforts to line his pocket with money from gullible tourists." I flashed my cynical smile again, and they returned to discussing their week's itinerary.

Before leaving I offered advice on three things they should enjoy before leaving Key West. "Take the Conch Train tour, because there's no better way to see the city, and by all means visit my friend, Mel Fisher's Treasure Museum. A couple of hours before sundown go to Mallory Square, because every famous person from Hollywood will be there at one time or another, as will former presidents and the super-rich. Drums will begin beating the sun down as some of the best performers entertain you in hopes that you will support their lifestyle with donations." With that, I bid everyone goodbye and wished them a fun-filled stay on the Isle of Bones.

When I closed the main salon door and headed toward the plush gangplank that had teak over polished bronze handrails and a very fancy carpeted walkway, I heard Jean-Philippe Doliscat softly call my name. "Hello, Jean-Philippe." I waved as he walked from the bow.

I had known the Haitian chef for about fifteen years. He has worked for my friend twice that long, shuttling between three mansions and two super-yachts. There is no greater contrast in black and white than when Jean-Philippe smiles, which he was doing as he approached.

"I didn't know you were aboard or I would have come to the galley. I thought you would be off shopping this early."

He embraced me saying, "It's always a pleasure to see you, Mister Py."

"For me too, Jean-Philippe."

"I just wanted to remind you Py, that all the voodoo dolls and the shoofly voodoo sticks can hear every bad word spoken about them. That Robert is maybe the most feared voodoo doll ever been, and he is for sure the most evil, so you must be very careful when you talk about him."

"I recall you telling me that a long time ago, Jean-Philippe. I'm getting old and forgetting things." I smiled at him, "Thank you for reminding me Jean-Philippe, I'll be more careful."

As I wiped the coffee cup dry and returned it to the cabinet, I thought about what Jean-Philippe had said just a few months earlier. *I guess,* I thought, *that might explain that little scenario that unfolded in here last night.* I stopped a moment and thought about that day I visited the Yacht he worked on. *How did Jean-Philippe know I had been talking about Robert the Doll that day? He had been all the way back in the stern a deck down preparing food for his boss's party that evening.* How he knew still puzzles me.

"Well," I said loudly, "ain't a darn thing I can do about it now."

I checked my tide chart to be certain I had read it correctly, and also had the right day and month. After computing time, wind, and speed, I knew I had plenty of time to fix breakfast, so I got out one of those beautiful snook filets. While they were frying I made a pot of yellow grits with some chicken broth I had left. I turned the snook and added some cheese to the grits, and then cracked three eggs into a bowl. After the diced onion and garlic were added I started stirring it all together in the bowl, and then poured it all into the hot butter in my new omelet skillet. Once the bottom was lightly browned I added a handful of shredded cheese and carefully eased it to the side of the skillet so I could turn it over with my Teflon spatula. By the time the omelet was on my plate, the coffee quit perking, so I poured a big cupful and headed toward the Captain's chair.

With a good breakfast under my ever-expanding belt, I went to the engine room and fired up the Lister. After walking all the way around the decks to visually see everything near the boat and in my area, I returned to the wheelhouse and began bumping the toggle-switch to bring the anchor up. Once the plow was on the bowsprit and locked, I headed Floating Homestead toward the familiar docks at Flamingo.

3

Old Pal—New Stories

DURING THE PREVIOUS EVENING, I'D THOUGHT about a good, long-time pal of mine that I hadn't visited for about three years. Eddie Sawyer was about my age. He was born in Key West, making him a true Conch. Many folks that have lived in the Florida Keys for many years refer to themselves as 'Conchs' but if they weren't born in Key West, then they're about as much true Conch as Obama is true American. As my old Kentucky granny was fond of saying, 'Just because you got off the bus at Hollywood and Vine doesn't mean you're a movie star.'

All of Eddie's nine brothers, and one sister, were born in Key West, and all but Eddie still live and work there.

Eddie got a job running a big mullet net-boat out of Flamingo back in the 40s and liked it there.

Actually I believe Eddie's a few years older'n me, so even though he's in pretty good shape, Eddie isn't gonna be around a heckuva lot longer. I spotted him driving the mower toward the docks and waving to me, so I knew that he'd already spotted me, and ain't any doubt who's coming once you've seen my boat.

When he had my lines on the cleats, I climbed up outa the boat and shook his hand. "Y'busy today?"

"Nope," he answered, "just finished mowin a chunk I couldn't git to yestiddy on account o' dark came too fast. Ain't gonna do a thing for a coupla days."

"Good deal," I answered, "we can spin a few yarns around a fire and lie about the fish we caught."

"Not me, Py," he shot a stream of tobacco juice at a big sheephead on the surface next to a piling, "I got pitchers o' the big'ns I've caught lately."

I grinned, "Still milking that thirty-seven pound snook you caught during my last visit?"

"Thet big ole hoss was converted a few days after you left, Py."

"Converted?" I asked with a frowning question mark on my face, "To what?"

"Turds." He laughed, and snorted through his long crooked nose.

"Darn, Eddie, you can sure ruin a fella's appetite."

He glanced at my protruding belly, "Not fer very long, though."

The breeze was still stout that evening and coming off the water, so we had a nice fire out behind his cabin. When the big mullet boom began tapering off, Eddie went to work for the Florida State Park as grounds keeper. He was allowed to move into one of the new cabins built for future Park Rangers and has lived in it ever since. He had his diploma from the Key West High School, so he began studying to take the State Ranger test. Ten years later he graduated thirteenth in a class of forty-one, and hasn't left Flamingo but about six times since.

Eddie's knowledge of the Everglades, the animals that live in it and the surrounding waters, plus every species that swims in the nearby bay waters and rivers, has made him a valuable asset to the park administration. Age limits have been waived and they all hope he stays right where he is.

"Eddie," I asked him that night, "what was that old man's name that had the biggest mullet operation that ever worked outa here?"

"Shores."

"Oh yeah, Bill Shores. I stopped and visited him some years back. I got his address up in Arcadia from one of his sons in Key Largo."

"Musta been ole Ralph."

"Yeah, it was. Great big mountain of a man. He was one of the gate guards for a condo community in Key Largo."

"He brung his wife over here n' stayed two days with me. He n' her quit drinkin after he got thet job." Eddie laughed and snorted through his nose again. "Ole Ralph was a wild man in his younger days. Tole me a coupla good stories I hadn't yet heard."

He poured me more iced tea and then topped off his. "His daddy wasn't religious when Ralph was younger. Ralph was the youngest o' them boys an stayed pretty close to home. He got in a travelin mood ever now n' then, an would take a berth on a shrimper or snapper boat goin across to the Campeche Banks off Mexico. One time, when Ralph was just a young guy, he kinda left his daddy in a fix. Went to Key West to buy a big ole mullet skiff an drive it back down here for Bill, 'cause he had a fella all set up to run it for him."

After a sip of tea, Eddie continued. "Ralph spent Bill's mullet boat money a'whorin around with all them Duval Street gals, an when he sobered up ole Ralph knew he was in deep poop. He got hisself a job on a snapper boat an didn't get back down here for about three months. Before he came here lookin for his daddy, Ralph stopped at the Last Chance Bar up on AIA, just before you hit the stretch leadin on down to Key Largo."

"Yeah, I know where it is, but never been inside."

Eddie chuckled, "I shouldn't laugh, because it was a pretty bad scene that changed Ralph's life. He was sittin there at the bar when Bill walked in with a tow chain about six foot long with the end coiled around one of those big hands of his."

I interrupted to say, "That was the first thing I noticed about Bill. His hands were about the size of an outfielder's baseball glove."

Eddie just sorta snorted, "Yeah, an they're chock full o' steel. Anyway, he stormed over to Ralph who didn't even know he was there. The first time he knowed his daddy had found him was when that chain hit Ralph up side the head. Went through the rest of his life with only one eye." Eddie turned to see me staring at him with my eyelids all scrunched down. "Didn't know one of his eyes was glass, didja Py?"

"I sure didn't. Musta been a good doctor that did the surgery."

"Ralph wore a patch for a few years until one day down in Mexico, a doctor he was drinkin with told him about a doctor friend of his in Juarez thet specialiced in puttin glass eyes in. Ever seen one, Py?"

"Nope."

"They're way bigger'n you think." He chuckled again, "I know of two times, an hard tellin how many more, when thet eye would be popped out n' tossed in his glass of beer to impress the girls. Ole Ralph would forget about it an swallow the dang thing. He had to poop through a screen ever time until he got the eye back." By this time Eddie was full-out laughing, and so was I.

Once he was settled down, Eddie asked, "Didja know Bill was a bare knuckle fighter?"

"Nope, but I can sure believe it."

"He fought all over Florida an was even thinkin about traveling all around the country fightin guys when he was younger. Had hisself way over a hunert matches an was never whupped once. In them days, Py, a fight went on till one guy couldn't git up fer the next round. Them fellers regularly fought a hunert rounds or more."

"Phewee," I shook my head, "he musta been one very tough guy to step into the ring with."

"He was, an he knew it, Py. He was known from end to end n' side to side in Florida as the toughest fighter in the state. He had a good pal named Cullen who lived in Key Largo. Can't recall his first name, but he n' ole Bill traveled all over the state to get fights. Cullen was listenin to the radio once when a fighter in Jacksonville claimed that Bill Shores was all mouth, an he was juss a'waitin for a chance to shut it up for him, once n' for all."

Eddie looked over at me and grinned, "Didn't hafta wait too long, 'cause when Cullen told ole Bill the guy's name they climbed in the car an headed north. I can still recall how Cullen gave me a blow-by-blow of thet fight."

'Bill ducked the first punch the guy threw and went in under his swing to lift the guy off the ground with a hard uppercut. I knew it was gonna be a battle when the guy bounced right back up and popped Bill on the jaw with a hard left hook. About ten rounds later neither of 'em looked like they had tired a bit. Bill knew how to get inside a tough fighter's fists, and this guy was dern sure a tough'n. Bill would stay low and inside punishing the guy's guts. Fifty-one rounds and Bill hadn't been knocked down once, but the other guy, I don't remember his name, had been flattened three times. Bill had the best flat-foot, square-on, right punch of anyone I ever saw. He never twisted and cocked his arm, he just stood there facing the opponent and when he saw an opening coming, he fired that right arm like it was cocked with a stick of dynamite behind it. Somewhere between ninety and a hunert of them rounds Bill flattened the guy twice with a pair of those. Round a hunert n' nine Bill hit him so hard that he was flat on his back trying to understand what had happened. The guy couldn't get up, so the referee pointed at Bill and yelled, "The winner." Me n' Bill had to get back to work because the mullet were really runnin and chock full of roe. I got all of the fight money while Bill was in showering off. Me n' Bill was soon headin back south."

Eddie and I sat there enjoying the skeeter-free evening until about midnight, and then went fishing the next day. By early afternoon I had enough speckled trout and snook filets in my freezer to last quite a while. The tide was high at 4:00 PM, so Eddie pushed me away from the dock and I headed out into the bay. I was soon heading west toward Chokoloskee, but stopped before dark and anchored the boat.

Lying in the bunk that night I thought about som'n Eddie told me the previous night.

"Py, I ain't never tole anyone, but since you're heading to Chokoloskee to write about ghosts, I'll tell you a coupla true stories. I was sittin right over there 'neath that big ole palm," he pointed toward a coconut palm near the water about fifty feet from his cabin, "when I saw the figure of a person begin to move. At first I thought it was someone gettin out of a skiff he'd beached, but a moment later I could see who it was." Eddie turned toward me and stared hard; to see, I suppose, if I was gonna laugh or say som'n stupid. He finally continued, "It was Bill Shores walkin right past me, Py. Ain't been no mullet fishing around here for quite a while, but the apparition kept walking back an forth where the drying racks for them cotton nets used t'be. After five or mebbe ten minutes, an I was a'watchin Bill ever dern minute he was nosin around them racks, he walked right on by me again an simply disappeared into the ground fog."

The next story he told made the hairs on the back of my neck stand up.

"I ain't never tole anyone this next story neither, Py." Eddie looked out across the water a long time before continuing. "I reckon when a person gits old as I am they can tell about things they did or saw, an it won't matter, 'cause they ain't gonna be around long enough for it to matter whether folks believe 'em or not.

This was back when I was runnin one of them big airboats for Bill Shores, that he built. I musta had about two ton o' mullet on that sucker, an the net too, but we was up on top a'flyin. Ole Bill n' I had completely rebuilt a big Packard motor to power it. Other guys was burning up motors left an right a'trying to push them heavy flatboats like Bill's, but there was som'n Bill done thet made his run hard all year and their's not more'n a trip or two. He got som'n called a thruss bearing, from some big industrial plant I reckon, an then rigged it to go on the flywheel between it n' the huge airplane perpeller. "

Eddie wiggled around in the chair a bit, and then looked around to be sure we were alone. "Like I said, Py, I was up on top n' flyin, when all of a sudden thet dern Packard juss quit. I sat there a moment tryin to remember if I'd topped off the fuel tanks, checked the oil, or mebbe did som'n to make her juss quit runnin like thet. After thinkin about all that stuff, I knew it wasn't som'n I did or forgot t'do, so I began figuring out about where I was. I struck thet last big school o' mullet about two hours before dark. The weather'd been kinda crappy an a fog bank was movin t'ord us, but we ran thru 'em all the time, so warn't no worry. We got all them fish outa thet net before dark, an had run flat out long enough thet I figgered us to be only a coupla miles from Flamingo. Problem was, we's sittin dead in the water.

I asked Parker Hamilton, the young boy who went with me to pick mullet outa the net, 'cause he was short like me n' could work back there under the motor, if he'd heard any odd sounds a'comin outa the motor. He said it was runnin great with no extra noise until it juss quit. We sat there a while bein as quiet as possible so we'd hear another boat if one was a'comin t'ward us. It warn't but mebbe fifteen minutes after thet Packard stopped runnin when we heard water a'splashin. I was kinda sick at my stomach thinkin about all them purdy mullet gonna be wasted if I couldn't figger out some way to get into Flamingo.

I had turned off the lights so the batteries would still roll the Packard over later to see if it'd start. I flipped 'em on an just a minute later a big ole sailboat went slowly pass us not three dern feet away. It was big as these newfangled shrimpers, Py, an was about twenty men standin there a'lookin down at us the whole time it passed."

Eddie paused and slowly shook his head back and forth. After a moment he looked at me, and then turned his eyes back toward the water and ran his hand through his hair a few times before continuing. "I still have a hard time believin it was all real, an Parker never went out on the water again." He turned to me, "Py, thet boy never tole a soul as far as I know. He went back up the road to Homestead about a month after thet ghost boat sailed through our lights. He entered school again, but thet night out there musta weighed heavy on him. In the same month he woulda gradjeated with a high school diplomer Parker took sick with som'n an didn't last a week."

Eddie was silent for a long time, just looking out across that dark expanse of water. Finally he said, "Py, them was the most pitiful lookin folks I ever laid eyes on. Warn't like them mean lookin pirates in magazines and funny papers. They all had a look o' sadness I ain't never seen before or after. I've had a hard time keepin 'em outa my daily thoughts ever since, so I reckon Parker juss warn't able to come to grips with it n' passed on. I shore hope he was able to leave all them haunting thoughts behind."

I sat quietly beside him in the dark sipping my tea. After ten or so minutes Eddie said, "I hit the starter button again, an thet ole Packard fired right up. Before striking thet last school, we already put the mullet we picked earlier in the ice boxes, an I knew it was gonna be a short run in. I told Parker not t'mess with them last mullet what was still in the net, because we was a'headin in while the Packard was runnin. I sometimes wonder, Py, if greed ain't got som'n to do with things like thet. We had a dern good load before I decided to strike thet last school. If I hadn't, thet dern Packard juss mighta run us right on into Flamingo, an young Parker'd still be with us."

I didn't know what to say, so I sat silently beside Eddie for a long ten or fifteen minutes, but then finally told him I was gonna pull out pretty early. I stood and stretched my back a few times before shaking his hand, and promising to stop by again fore too long.

That darn story stuck in my mind all the way along the coast. I got well beyond Chatham Bend before anchoring for the night. I knew the Park Rangers had burned down Mister Watson's house a few years earlier, for some stupid reason I'll never understand, but I really didn't wanna be anchored close to the place. I'd already heard enough about ghosts to know they can be awfully cantankerous at times.

After a dinner of fried snook filets and yellow grits, I opened the hatch and climbed up to the roof and opened my chair. It wasn't yet dark but getting close, so when I heard the k'chuk, k'chuk, k'chuk of a one lung engine, I searched the area for a boat. Nothing, but I could still hear that engine quite clearly. It was the same kind of engine that was in Mister Watson's launch, so I sorta expected him to come alongside soon and ask for some matches or som'n. When the sound got fainter and fainter, I figured out it was heading toward Key West, whatever it was. I laid in my bunk until the wee hours thinking about the ghost project, and wondered if it was gonna be as much fun as I at first thought it would.

4

Chokoloskee Island

*T*HE TIDE WAS ALMOST HIGH BY THE TIME I GOT Floating Homestead up alongside the dock pilings behind the old Smallwood Trading Post & Museum.

After securing the boat and checking everything in the engine room, I stepped onto the dock. I had already been told that the Smallwood Museum was still closed, until a court decided what to do. The asphalt-paved road, Mamie Street, that ran into the Smallwood Trading Post, which is a one-hundred-year-old historical building, and is also documented as part of the public domain, had just been ripped out. Apparently it was because a land developer from up the coast a good ways in Sebring didn't want the public driving to and from the museum on *'his'* road, which incidentally was named for the trading post's current proprietor's grandmother, Mamie Smallwood. I was a bit surprised to see the signs and fence wire still surrounding the entire area preventing the public from visiting the museum. *Looks kinda like a damned concentration camp around here now than a museum site.*

For Christ's sake, I thought as I looked around, *the guy musta bought this entire end of Chokoloskee.* I cut through the swamp, which was the only way to get in or out, since the brat had fenced off the way out as well as the way in. It was low tide, but the water was still ankle-deep in a path that led through the swamp to the next road, which is Calusa Drive.

I sloshed through the swamp, cussing that Sebring brat all the way, and I doubt I'm the first to do that. I walked up Calusa toward the Post Office that shared the same building as The Havana Café. Fisherman friends who had eaten there said the food was excellent, so by the time I got there, that snook filet I had for breakfast was ready to be converted. I had a good inner chuckle every time I thought of Eddie's idea about converting food.

I exited the men's room and sat at one of the small tables. The owner/chef was busy filling orders brought to him by young waitresses that I later learned were his wife and daughters. Watching the middle-aged Cuban filling plates, left no doubts that he was not a newcomer to the food business. Everything that passed by me in the hands of his servers smelled great, and looked like too much for the average guy or gal to consume.

I walked in thinking about a nice hot Cuban sandwich

and a small cup of thick, black, sweet Cuban coffee, but the recent food conversion process had left me weak. The adorable young waitress scribbled frantically as I rattled off a list of my favorites. "Picadillo, rice, fried plantains, a couple of slices of Cuban toast, Cuban coffee for now, and some iced tea with the meal, please." Before she got away, I asked if they had flan, and when she said they made the custard every day, I ordered it. I once waited to order flan at a restaurant in Miami until I finished my meal. "Sorry," the waiter said, "just sold the last one." I never forgot it.

An hour later I waddled up the road toward Viking Country. I had met Ray McMillin a few years earlier when I was in Everglades City for the annual Seafood Festival. It's one of the biggest and best in the state, and fills the area with aircraft, motorhomes, boats, cars, motorcycles, and tour busses on the first full weekend in February.

Ray was at WinCar Hardware, that day a few years earlier, and was talking to Jim Webb, the store owner. Jim introduced us, and Ray invited me to go mullet fishing with him that afternoon. Later that day we brought in some of the best looking west coast black mullet I'd ever seen, and also the biggest.

I helped prepare 'em, and then watched as his son, Gary, put them all in his smoker. I've eaten smoked mullet up and down the Florida West Coast, but never had any as good as those that Gary-Mac pulled out of that converted wooden chill-barrel that once sat on the deck of his fifty-foot long, tunnel-drive, trap-boat.

After he finished covering the box with croaker sacks, so the smoldering buttonwood smoke would cook the two dozen mullet during the next three or four hours, with regular peeks inside by Gary, we climbed into his pickup truck and drove up to his house. I said up, because the house sits atop columns on a shell mound high enough to easily be considered a real hill on Chokoloskee.

When I had earlier asked about the fence and tarps that surrounded the Smallwood Trading Post, Gary said I would hafta talk to his wife, Lynn. "Py, I have my hands full just keeping the boat in tiptop shape n' ready to take out the next charter." He turned toward me and grinned after stopping in his asphalt driveway, "I stay away from there as much as I can. A boatload o' people now n' then's enough socializing for me."

I learned later that quite a few of the larger stone crab trap-boat operators like Gary had shut down. All had similar answers to my question, "Why?"

One of 'em said, "It's pretty damn common these days, after y'go out there n' pull a thousand o' yer traps, then after payin the crew, the fuel bill, and make a few repairs, to learn thacha lost money that day. And then before y'know it, the annual stone-crab-trap-tag bill is due, and brother, the Green Gestapo says y'gotta put a tag on every darn trap, *that you built*." He almost screamed those last three words."

This guy was trapping stone crabs for forty years before he quit and went back into construction work. He shook his head, "Add several thousand dollars for bait," he raised his eyebrows to look at me above his glasses, "that we usta get for a coupla cents a pound and at times free because they wanted to get that rotten stuff outa their way." He slowly shook his head side-to-side, "And then you realize that you'd worked all week for nothing, and occasionally you actually lost money that week."

He went on to tell me how much each trap cost by the time it had a concrete bottom poured in it, with a line and buoy attached, plus a tag screwed to the top.

As I strolled along the road following the Barron River in Everglades City, where the commercial trapping boats were docked near the fish houses they supply during the season, I wondered, *maybe the greedy government geeks are setting it all up so locals can't afford to trap. Then they can lease the bottom out to foreign ships.* I walked on toward Triad, the best fresh retail seafood counter that I had found in the area—and a great restaurant too. It sits right on the Barron River, so you can see the airboats passing by, and at times alligators, manatees, pelicans, and many other critters that consider the Everglades home.

I sat at one of the picnic tables in the Triad Restaurant and Retail Seafood breezeway. As soon as a waitress, from the screened in dining room sitting on poles out over the water, came out, I waved.

"Hi," she waved back, "be right there, as soon's I put in this order."

A few minutes later I was eating the best shrimp gumbo I've ever tasted. "Hey, Py, that rusty old bike you're pumping must be the one you bought at the thrift store."

I turned, but already knew by the Immokalee-Cracker drawl, that it was Orlo, the owner of Triad. "Yep, best dern ten bucks I've spent in a while."

"You slimin down so you can go trolling for one o' those hot little Chokoloskee cupcakes?"

"Nope, I'm just out enjoying the fresh air. Besides, one cupcake, hot or cold, would put me in ICU. Hell's Belles, I got a nice comfortable old pancake in Key West, and I only stop by to see her every coupla months."

"Gittin old, huh?"

"Like the song says, Orlo, I ain't as good as I once was, but I'm as good once as I ever was."

"You stayin on your boat at the Smallwood Trading Post dock?"

"Yeah, Lynn gave me a key so I can go up inside during the evening to see if there's anything to all these stories circulating about ghosts up there rattling chains n' makin a buncha noise."

The sun was getting low as I pedaled back across the causeway from Everglades City. I pumped on past the Post Office toward Chokoloskee Drive and turned right then sailed along nicely on the asphalt until I reached the corner. I stopped the bike and looked across the street at Totch Brown's big house. I got off the bike then to look over the temporary fence at the sorry mess on both sides of Mamie Drive. *Lynn McMillin's grandma,* I thought as I looked at the destroyed road, *probably turned over in her grave when she saw that.* After letting my eyes roam across the entire area, I thought, *Ted Smallwood probably did too.*

It was put in 100 years ago to lead to his trading Post, and years later was paved to lead tourists to it. It never resembled the Autobahn that runs through Germany, but it was a very serviceable, asphalt-paved road leading to the Smallwood Trading Post until that twerp came down from Sebring, Florida with his collection of Tonka trucks and tore it out.

I peddled back to Calusa Drive and headed toward the path through the swamp. I tried riding but remembered how I almost fell earlier when I tried riding across that mulch. So, I stopped the bike and got off and pushed it the rest of the way—cussing that spoiled little jerk from Sebring all the way.

A half-hour before the sun dropped into the Gulf of Mexico I chained the bicycle to one of the wooden pilings that supports the Smallwood Trading Post. Standing underneath a few minutes looking out across the bay at the barrier islands, I thought, *this musta been paradise for the pioneers once they learned how to control the mosquitos and other critters around here.* I then climbed aboard Floating Homestead and went down into my aluminum cave.

This was my sixth night at the trading post's dock. I had unlocked the place a few days earlier and walked around upstairs. It had been several years since I'd been inside but nothing had changed much—well, one thing was missing.

I had already been told that Mister Watson, the big tomcat that had laid claim to an area on the counter, right beside the only entrance, had finally tired of everyone disturbing him with pats on the head, 'nice kitty-kitty' and other human chatter. After several years as a tolerant greeter, purring had been replaced with growls and an occasional swipe at the offending hand of the many unwelcome admirers. He soon found a new home as the replacement of a recently deceased cat that left an older woman painfully devastated—until Barbara Lewinski, the local guardian angel to cats and other animals, introduced her to Mister Watson. He now enjoys life thoroughly as a gentleman cat that gets everything he wants—without putting up with visitors disturbing him during nap-time.

I sat up there in the dark, even though I could have flipped on the lights. Most of the 'true' tales I had read about ghosts indicated that they preferred darkness to do their chain-rattling, furniture-moving, and spooky woooo act to impress, intimidate, or frighten humans—who had not yet become ghosts themselves.

At midnight I awoke from a brief snooze and flipped on the bright LED flashlight that I had with me.

A slow search along the west side of the west wing the life-size acrylic replica of Ted Smallwood caught my eye. He was sitting in his old rocker since Lynn had a firm in Ft. Myers create it. My flashlight search yielded no ghosts or spooky shadows moving across the walls. I walked right past Ted and searched the small room that was once the Post Office—still no ghostly stuff.

Exiting the west wing via an opening in the middle, I stopped in the central area, which is the original, and was the only part of the building until Ted raised it and positioned it on wooden poles. He later added the two wings to expand it for storage of items he knew the local pioneers and Indians would need.

Shining the light across the walls full of original stock, I still saw nothing that caused me to think that ghosts had been frolicking about with their rattling chains and other man-fear paraphernalia.

I moved through the east opening and turned left to go check the small bedroom and toilet—still no ghost stuff. I moved back to where I had been sitting for a short snooze, and shined the light on the door that led to the storage room where kerosene and tools were kept. Unlatching the upper half, I shoved it back and opened the bottom half. The light illuminated both ends easily, and still there was nothing to make me believe that ghosts had been using the trading post as a gathering place.

After latching both of the storage doors again I walked slowly toward the huge barn-type door that opened out onto the porch. I leaned against the railing and looked down at my boat. As a precaution I shined the light from bow to stern and was glad there were no signs of ghostly movement there either.

After locking the doors to the porch, I locked the front door and headed down the stairs. My thoughts as I went down were still, *this ghost thing is simply a human-fear-fire in a person's mind, which once lit burns wild through the mind of weak people near enough to hear its flames crackling and decide to join in.*

~ O ~

A dark night in the near future would radically alter my attitude about the thought of ghosts that I never feared—until I met Robert the Doll.

At the bottom of the steps I walked around the east end of the huge old building and headed toward my boat.

It was lying against the telephone poles that supported the outer part of the wooden dock. There wasn't a breeze to make the boat pound as it bumped against the pilings, so I stood on the dock a moment trying to figure out what was causing the boat to be doing just that—*bump, bump, bump.*

It was a bright full-moon night, and my eyes quickly became adjusted during the short walk around to Floating Homestead. The boat was so motionless that if the tide had not been high, I would have thought it was sitting on the muddy bottom. I heard the *bump, bump, bump* again, but it was so slight and muffled that I couldn't quite pinpoint the location. It was not caused by the boat though, of that I was certain.

I leaned against the piling, so even my clothes or shoes would not be crinkling or squeaking. I silently awaited the return of the bump, bump, bump.

Ten minutes later I stepped aboard, having convinced myself that the noise was in my head. *Maybe,* I thought, *it's just a gear or som'n inside my brain that got rusty and isn't turning smoothly.* Moving forward, I pulled down the two stepping-pegs, and holding the rail that surrounded the gas bottles and entry hatch, I stepped up onto the roof.

After opening the hatch and lowering the ladder, I went down two treads and stopped. After a long five minutes it was still so quiet that I could hear the ice cream in the freezer calling me, but there was still no bump, bump, bump. One last glance at the old building, and I pulled the hatch to me and went on down.

That bump, bump sound was so darn spooky, that once I had secured the hatch and shoved the ladder back up, I stood there another five minutes listening—still not a sound except the boat sounds that I was used to.

After a dish of ice cream, I stretched out on my bunk to read a few pages of Carl Hiaasen's book, Kick Ass. I had a few good chuckles while reading this collection of his old columns written for the Miami Herald, but was so tired on this night, that after a few paragraphs of his February 27th 1994 column, 'Alpha 66 threats', I dropped off to sleep with the heavy book on my chest.

*Bump, bump, bump...*it woke me from a sound sleep. I lay there wondering if I had imagined it, or perhaps my brain was doing reruns of the earlier noise. My bunk reading light was a small LED at the tip end of a flexible shaft, so I reached up and turned it off.

Pressing the stem on my Timex, a light informed me that I had been sleeping for over three hours, because it was just a few minutes before four o'clock in the morning.

I lay there in the dark for what seemed a long time, but when I heard that *bump, bump, bump* again, I pressed the stem on the Timex—4:13.

I swung my feet out and eased into a sitting position on the narrow bunk. My toes found the slippers and once all twelve of them were tucked inside the fur-lined moccasin-like house slippers...(right, twelve. Double little toes on each hoof)—I silently stood.

I never close the door to my small stateroom, so I was comfortable stepping into the dark interior of my floating home. By the time old eyes were adjusted to the faint light coming into the boat through the front window and the 10" bronze portholes along both sides of the cabin, I coulda seen any movement. *Nobody could get in here,* I thought as I moved toward the stern.

I stood perfectly still and listened for any movement in the engine room on the other side of the bulkhead. I knew the topside hatch leading down into the engine room was closed and locked. But I was still listening for movement on the other side, and my mind was working overtime. *The thief, if there is one, would hafta open all four dogs on this waterproof door, and by then,* I almost said aloud while leaning toward the narrow, 60" oval door, *he'd be looking down the barrel of my gun.*

I was still standing there, considering opening the oval door to the engine room anyway, when the noise bounced through the portholes. It was louder than previously, and seemed to be originating up inside the trading post.

Bump, bump, bump. I stood motionless for a brief moment, but when the noise came again, and much louder, I walked toward the stairs and pulled them down. *Whatever the heck is making that noise, ghosts or a buncha smart aleck kids, I'm not gonna sit in here wondering.*

After releasing the latch, I shoved the hatch up while holding the rope until it was in place. Stepping onto the roof I held the rope as the hatch went on back until it rested against the rail that partitioned the propane tanks from the hatch.

I stood and leaned against the rail as my eyes did a scan of the museum's shuttered windows. At the end of the old building I began glancing up at the roof and then down beneath it to the west side pilings that it sat on. Just as I was moving my eyes back up to the roof, still hoping to see something—anything that might explain the bump, bump noise, my peripheral vision caught movement.

My head snapped around so quick my glasses almost flew off, and all that prevented it was the old fashioned set of wires that wrapped around my big ears. I held my breath and looked straight at the man who was looking down at me.

"Who are you?" I said it quietly, but when nothing to indicate that the man had heard me, I raised my voice a few octaves. **"I said who are you, and how in the heck didja get up on that porch?"** When the man just stared at me a moment, and then began drifting away like he was made of fog, my mouth dropped open.

Holy crap, I thought while watching that apparition on the porch slowly dissolve into thin air, *I could spot that big lug in a crowd. That was Ted Smallwood.*

After standing there next to the rail for half an hour to see if the apparition would reappear, I pulled the hatch to me and started down the folding stairs. Half way down I stopped and spent ten more minutes scanning the area. *I wonder if maybe I'm still asleep in my bunk, and all of this is just a dream?*

Shaking my head slowly, I continued down, pulling the hatch cover shut. After latching it, I shoved the steps back up into place, and climbed into the captain's chair.

I sat there looking at stars until the sun began chasing darkness from the sky. My mind was working hard to make some kind of sense of what I had seen, or thought I'd seen. *To hell with logic*, I thought, exiting the chair. *That was definitely not a product of my imagination. That was ole Ted Smallwood himself I saw.* I went to the galley and began digging through the fridge for breakfast makings. "I'm gonna have pancakes n' bacon," I said aloud, "then I'm gonna get myself some rest so I can spend tonight up there in the museum."

After breakfast I stacked the skillet and dishes in the sink and then set the timer on 5:30. Once I was stretched out on the bunk, I lay there with my fingers locked behind my head. My thoughts were a bit odd, *if that was Ted, and he shows up again tonight, then I'm gonna be ready to talk to him about ghosts, apparitions, spooks, or whatever the heck goes on over there on the other side.*

Before it got too dark to see without a flashlight, I went upstairs and got settled into a chair across from the one that the acrylic replica of Ted Smallwood was in. *I wonder what ole Ted thinks about when he sees som'n like that. I don't think I'd like to walk into a store after I've kicked the bucket, n' see m'self sittin there like a goldang freeze-dried Pinocchio.*

"Why?"

When I heard the voice my body automatically spun around so fast that I thought for a moment I'd busted something. I began rubbing my neck briskly while looking straight at the man who had just spoken. Ted Smallwood was standing behind the dummy in the chair.

"Why what?" The words just leaped out of my mouth.

"Why would you care what they did with your carcass if you were already dead?"

I just sat there staring at Ted as my mind tried to put the events of the past few moments into perspective. *This can't be real. Dead people can't talk to you. I must still be in bed, and I'm dreaming.*

"Y'ain't dreaming, son, dead people can talk to very specific people, but there must be a very good reason, otherwise the words just vaporize and can't be heard. I'm curious, mister, why would you or me or anybody care what was done to our body after the soul has gone on to Heaven?"

I cleared my throat, but before I could say a word, Mister Smallwood said, "I saw you on the funny looking boat sitting at my dock. By the way, what's your name?"

"Pyorrhea Lam, and it's only funny looking because most of the boats they're building these days are just toys.

Ted's brow furrowed a bit and one eyebrow rose as he looked hard at me. Finally he asked, "You got rotten teeth or infected gums?"

"Nope," I said a little to loudly, "my mom just liked the sound of that word."

Ted looked hard at me for a long moment before speaking. "I reckon a woman ought to be allowed to name her kids as she sees fit. And I agree with you about the new boats I've seen around here lately."

"I agree with you, Mister Smallwood, a...

He interrupted me to say, "Ted, just call me Ted."

"Okay, Ted, a woman probably experiences more pain delivering a baby than any man will ever feel, so she sure oughta be allowed to name her kids however she wants."

Ted said, "Yep." He chuckled, "About these new toy boats, I saw one just a while back run up on an oyster bar," he nodded east toward Lynn and Gary-Mac's property, "just a ways off my granddaughter and her husband's property. I heard that big ole motor screaming and watched him turn outa the channel and run right up on the bar. Warn't even low tide yet, but he sure tore a big chunk of the boats' bottom out." Ted shook his head slowly, "Coupla days later a barge with a crane came and loaded it. Looked like it was about twenty–five or mebbe thirty feet long, and so much of the bottom was gone, I doubt it was worth rebuilding."

"Ted, I've been living on that boat for over half a century, and wish now I had taken a picture of all the boats I've gone past that were already junk and just a few years old."

He just shook his head as if to say he had seen quite a

few too. "You're here to write about us ghosts that folks are talking about, aincha?"

"Yeah Ted, but now that I know it's actually true, I wanna tell everyone that reads the book why you're all meeting here at your old trading post."

There was a very long pause before he answered. "There's lots of reasons we've been gathering up here since that guy from Sebring closed it down. We're fed up with a lot of things that's been happening here on Chokoloskee Island—well, it ain't an island any longer, but we all still think of it as one."

He paused so I took the opportunity to ask, "Like what?"

"Seems like it started with them darn boats they put airplane motors on. Every time I drifted over towards Everglades City to see if they were getting any crabs or crawfish, one of those things came roaring down the river like some kind of outa control airplane." He shook his head of silver hair, "Loudest thing that ever ran through town, I reckon. A fella couldn't even hear himself think until it got on down the river a ways."

"I noticed," I said, "how loud they are while I was sitting by the river the other day. I was told they were forced to put mufflers and them new composite props on all the airboats to quiet 'em down. I can sure remember how loud they were before."

Ted huffed, "Wasn't to make 'em quiet, Py, it was to put a wad of money in some pockets. Them contraptions are dern near as loud's they ever were. But once you let som'n like those boats start lining the pockets of a few people with dollar bills, you're stuck with 'em. I look for 'em to be carrying tourists out to the barrier islands for picnics right across from my trading post, before too long."

I heard a noise that reminded me of a blue heron or a crane flapping its wings to land. Ted heard it too because his head swiveled like mine toward the closed central door opening onto the porch. A moment later three men passed right through the door.

"That's C. G. McKinney, Adolphus Santini, and Juan Gomez from Panther Key."

"That's odd to name a Key like that," I said, "panthers on it back then?"

Ted turned and looked at me like I was some kind of New York City first-time visitor to Florida. "It was named that after a panther swam across and ate old man Gomez' goat."

"Santini," I said, "was the fella who got into a fight with Mister Watson in Key West, wasn't he?"

"Yeah," Ted said quietly, "Edgar cut his throat a bit and ole Adolphus never forgot it. He was probably more responsible for what happened to Edgar than DD House or anybody else." Ted chuckled a bit before adding, "Edgar bought a mule that same year and named it Dolphus. Santini fumed about that ever after—even to this day, I reckon."

"What'll happen if Edgar shows up while Santini is here?"

Ted turned to me with a wide smile, "Ever seen two ghosts fight?"

I didn't know what to say. "Can't happen, can it?"

"Don't know much about the world of ghosts, do you, Py?"

"Nope, but I can't picture a coupla ghosts duking it out."

"If Edgar floats in while Santini's here, then keep your eyes open."

As I watched the three men—ghosts—kinda float toward us, I tried to picture two of 'em goin' at it. Couldn't imagine it, but then I looked at Ted, and he seemed as whole and real as anybody that I had talked to lately. "What if Mister Watson shows up and has that shotgun with him?"

"He'd still have them two empty wet shells in both of the barrels, but even if they were good he couldn't do anything with it. I don't really know if he died with it still in his hands, but if he did then it'll be with him if he ever stops by, but he can't shoot or do anything else with it."

"You haven't seen him since that day?"

"Nope, none of us around here have seen him." Ted was silent a moment, but then added, "Can't blame him, it wasn't a good day for Edgar."

I was still curious. "He couldn't float in like those guys," I nodded at the other three who had stopped and were looking at something behind the counter, "and start shooting to vent some rage?"

"Ha," Ted snorted, "he might want to because they did him wrong that day as far as I'm concerned, but in our ghostly world it doesn't work that way. I've rattled a few chains, like the time a boy was dragging a dog on a choker-chain going past the graveyard. It took all the mental willpower I could muster to get that chain off the dog's neck so I could suspend it in front of that brat and shake it. Reckon I scared a few years off the end of his life, but it left me so weak I couldn't float up out of the coffin I spend most of my time in, for a year."

I was surprised, "So ghosts can't go around rattling chains and moving things around at will, huh?"

"Maybe some can, but not me or anyone around here that I know. Takes a powerful surge of energy to do anything like that and then later on it's as though your batteries are deader'n a doornail for a long time."

"How about the many stories I've read about pirate ghosts whacking an arm off someone with a cutlass? A ghost pirate in India supposedly cut off the arms of a hundred people back in the sixteenth century."

"Malarkey," Ted huffed out, "look here." He raised his arm and chopped down on my arm so fast I didn't react fast enough to prevent it. But then I saw that his arm and hand just whooshed thru my arm like a cloud would. "If that tale is true, then it was a real live fella getting even with some folks he figured had done him wrong, or else he was just plain crazy."

A hard thunderstorm had been rumbling its way toward us ever since I come upstairs. Probably the loudest crack of lightning I ever heard let loose and it seemed like it musta hit right close. I looked at Ted and he was as calm and unconcerned as a cadaver in a coffin. About the time I started to say som'n, another blast of lightning and thunder shook the trading post. Ted was looking at a six foot long diamondback rattlesnake mounted on a board and hung up on the wall leading into his old Post Office. I just happened to be looking toward the huge closed door, that when opened was access onto the rear porch, when another loud crack of lightning and thunder shook the hundred year old building again. As simultaneous as if it was created in a movie studio, Edgar J. Watson was standing just inside the doorway.

Even sitting where I was, which was right across from the acrylic replica of Ted Smallwood, I knew immediately that it was Mister Watson. He was wearing a wide-brim hat and had that long black frock over his clothes. It hung down to the top of his work boots, which I saw when he strode with confidence right past the others and said hello to Ted.

"That your twin brother, Mister Smallwood?" Edgar nodded toward the dummy with a sly smile on his face.

"Hello Edgar," Ted nodded a greeting, "do y'reckon he's as stately and handsome as I am?"

"Don't reckon there was ever a man on Chokoloskee that even came close to you." Edgar leaned against the passageway post. "I suppose there mighta been one," his handsome face opened into a wide smile, "but then I was always just a visitor up from my plantation on Chatham Bend."

"And that was a humble planter," Ted said with an obvious twinkle in his eye, "that few took notice of."

Edgar looked straight at me, "And who might you be, sir?"

Before I could answer, Ted spoke. "He's a writer and was sent here by his editor to write a story about us ghosts gathering here to frighten these newfound tourists who have come to visit our island."

"Well, by golly," Edgar said loudly with a stomp of his boot, "we'll sure give you one." His still unlit cigar had not glowed red for over a hundred years, but a moment later a small white ghost came billowing out his mouth. I figured that must have been the last puff he had before a vigilante posse gunned him down, right below where we sat.

Edgar chomped down on the cigar and turned toward the men he had just moved past. In a fluid motion as he turned, his hand casually moved his frock back, revealing a huge pistol in a holster resting on his hip.

"Good day CG," he nodded, "hello Mister Gomez, howdy Dolphus, ooops, Adolphus I mean—sorry." Edgar leaned forward, "That scar on your throat never did heal right, did it?"

Without a word, Adolphus Santini whooshed through the air and in a split second was through the door. "Still a thin-skinned, touchy ole bugger ain't he." Edgar snorted a laugh then walked into the cubbyhole that was once the local Post Office. Once back out he said, "Place sure has changed since last I was in here."

"You been over to Everglades City in the last few dozen years Edgar?"

"Nope, ain't been back in this area since that inbred buncha swamp-rat vigilantes murdered me."

"Seems t'me," Ted said, "that it was more like a well-planned suicide than a murder."

With a wave of his arm Edgar said, "Water over the dam."

The entire time that Ted and Edgar chatted, I was turning my attention from one to the other.

"Gonna have a crick in your neck tonight, Py." Edgar had a devilish but likeable grin on his face. The more I watched how he handled himself, the more I began to like this infamous character that had helped, albeit unaware, put this small shell mound on the tourist-destination map—both national and international.

"Nah," I answered, "I'll be too busy typing all this to notice a crick in my neck or a twist in my back."

Edgar grinned then turned to Ted, "I heard that while this trading post is closed up, a bunch of us old timers were gonna get together up here and see if we could come up with a plan to frighten the bad guys enough that they'll leave n' never come back down here."

Ted grinned, "We oughta be able to do that if you'll stick around a while, but I sure doubt if Adolphus will ever return."

Edgar just chuckled.

Ted then asked why they got in that fight down in Key West that ended with Edgar cutting Santini's throat—a wee bit, as Edgar once said with a smile, according to Ted.

"He accused me of messin with one of his wimmin. I tole him to stop telling folks that, because I didn't, and darn sure didn't want anyone I knew to think I would have anything to do with the kind of wimmin he was always taking up with down there on The Isle of Bones. He pulled his pocket knife out and waved it around."

Edgar paused a moment as though remembering the event. "Well, I showed that loudmouth what a real knife looked like, and then I just nicked his throat a bit so's he'd know I meant what I tole him." He laughed and added, "Ever after, if he was in Key West and heard I was comin, he'd lay low until I finished my business and headed home to Chatham Bend."

Ted said, "That's the exact same thing that ole Eddie Sawyer told me."

"Truth will always float to the top of a tub full of bull crap." Mister Watson turned to where C. G. McKinney and Juan Gomez were still talking, "Hey, I'm going down to Chatham and spend the night so I can look around in morning light to see what the old homestead looks like these days. You fellers wanna come along and have a looksee?"

Ted spoke up before either could answer. "Edgar, they burnt it to the ground."

The puzzled look that swept across Edgar's face was as though someone told him a flock of alligators just flew over the roof. He looked hard at McKinney and Gomez, and then he turned back to Ted. His mouth hung open and his eyebrows pulled down. Finally he asked, "They burnt it to the ground. Who in the hell is, they?"

Ted paused just a moment before softly saying, "The Everglades National Park Rangers."

In those few brief moments of ice-cold deathly silence immediately following Ted Smallwood's truthful but very shocking statement, I saw the killer that history says that Edgar Watson was.

Edgar reached up and removed his wide-brim hat, and then ran his fingers through his hair. His hat hand slowly went down to the side of his leg, and he leaned on the counter with the other hand and simply shook his head slowly back and forth. "Why in God's name are there a buncha rangers here in these swamps, and what would cause 'em to burn my house down?"

"I'm afraid I can't answer either of your questions with any logic, Edgar. I juss reckon them dern g'ment folks up in Washington wanted this land we call swamp for their own reasons, and I don't suppose nobody could ever give me a reason why they burned your house down." Ted just looked at Mister Watson and shook his head too.

I wasn't sure if I should speak or keep m'trap shut, but I ain't ever been one to keep quiet, even when I knew I should.

"Mister Watson...

Edgar interrupted me to say again, "Edgar, just plain Edgar."

...well Edgar," I continued, "land, whether it's mostly water or all sand, ain't being made any longer. If those crooked men in Washington see a large area they want, then proceedings are soon begun to make it a Federal Reserve. Down History's Road a hundred or so years, if they need a place to herd undesirables, they just rename the area a Federal Reservation. They'll then put a troop of Federal Police on the property to guard whoever they send there until they decide what to do with 'em. They did that to thousands of Japanese Americans who were loyal American Citizens, during World War Two."

"Well," Edgar said after a while, "I darn sure don't wanna go to Chatham just to see a blank chunk o' land where my big ole two-story house used to sit." He placed his hat back on and looked at Ted. "Mister Smallwood, when is this get-together up here s'posed to take place?"

"Independence Day weekend, Edgar, because I reckon most folks will be involved with family and won't be apt to come down here. Will you be coming back?"

"Yeah, Ted, I'd kinda like to face some of those fellers that filled me full of lead that day."

"Y'ain't gonna be startin trouble are you?"

"Nossir, Mister Smallwood, I just wanna remind 'em that there wasn't a lick of evidence linking me to any of them killings down at Chatham, and see what they have to say about that."

Ted linked his hands together under the straps of his overalls and looked at Edgar. "For what it's worth, Edgar, I never did think you killed them folks down there, and I told 'em so that day, but you know how a crowd gets when there's enough of 'em to make each frightened man among 'em feel safe."

"Yeah, I remember that day as though it happened an hour ago. I noticed Henry Short," he looked down at Ted who had pulled a chair out to sit on, "you remember Henry, doancha Ted, most called him Nigger Short. That was DD House's doing, but I always called him Henry."

"Anyways," Edgar continued, "I spotted Henry way over yonder on the left standing almost knee deep in the water and holding that nice rifle of his. We was eye-to-eye and I remembered som'n I had told him long before; 'when you know you have som'n t'do, Henry, don't back down dammit, just go ahead and do it.' A split second later he had his rifle up, and then the next split second I felt that slug hit me slap in the middle of m'forehead."

Mister Watson paused for a moment, and by the look in his eyes he was reliving that deadly event. "I remember turning toward the crowd, and as their slugs began hittin m'body I was able to take a wobbly step toward them. The double-barreled shotgun was still in my hands but the barrel was sagging down because my arms were no longer strong enough to hold it up." He laughed, "The damned buckshot was running out the end of the barrel.

A blink later I started down, but by then the shotgun had fallen from m'hands."

Ted spoke softly as he looked up at Edgar, "My wife Mamie didn't know anything about guns or ammunition. Later that day when someone said they saw the shot running out the barrels of your gun, I went to the cabinet where Mamie got those shells for you the last time you were here. They were the ones that got wet during a heavy rainstorm. I was gonna try to get reimbursed a little from the manufacturer and put 'em all in the second drawer. The new ones were in the top drawer, but I reckon Mamie didn't remember that I told her I'd moved all the fresh ammunition up to the top drawer." He looked up at Edgar and said, "I'm truly sorry."

"Ain't nothin t'be sorry about, Mister Smallwood, and sure wasn't Mamie's fault. I'd shaved down swollen shells before and never had a problem, so I musta shaved 'em down too much and they just started falling apart inside the barrel." He kinda let out a grunting sorta laugh, "Can't lay no blame at Henry Short's feet neither, 'cause he was only doing what I told him he should do. The House family took him right in when he was a kid and treated him good, especially him being the only Negro on the island. When he put that slug in my forehead he proved two things. One, he was the best damn shot on the island, and two, he's gonna look out for his family even if it was gonna cost him his life."

"Darn near did, too." Ted looked back up at Edgar, "There was several who said any nigger that would shoot a white man oughta be hanged straight away. Better minds prevailed, and all the folks who was talking about hanging Henry kept their mouths shut and went on about their business. Your body hadn't been lying on the beach, where the crowd carried it, for no time atoll when ole Henry up n' disappeared. Shows how smart he was. He took his small sailboat and went back down to Possum Key. Henry dismantled the dead Frenchman's old shack and moved it piece-by-piece all the way to West Cape Sable. Toted them boards on his back three miles inland to a grown up area where nobody coulda found him even if they did come lookin for 'that nigger that shot Mister Watson'."

"Well, that's good. Ain't no hard feelings atoll against Henry for shootin me that day. He was protecting the only family he ever had, and for good cause too, because I'd made up my mind that DD House was gonna get the first load of buckshot." He chuckled, "Never know how things are gonna turn out when a bunch of scared fellows like they was get their guns out."

"Mister Watson," I said, "I've been making notes. I hope you don't mind, because I'd like this article or book to be as authentic as possible."

"I don't mind atoll, Mister...uhhhh..."I told him again, "Py, just plain Pee why"... well Py," he continued, "I'd rather people know what really happened, so I'll look forward to seeing you again."

• • •

I was sitting on top of the store's new pellet-stove that hurricane water got into a few years earlier and ruined the auger motor that carries pellets into the flame. Ted Smallwood, DD House, and Erskine Thompson were sitting at the table beside the passageway between the original trading post and the west wing that Ted had added some years later.

It was early in the Saturday evening of Independence Day weekend of 2011. A few of the early settlers were gathered around the open passageway to the east wing, and others were standing near Totch Brown's pitty-pan, the tiny boat he'd made to carry the gator pelts that he'd poached out of the Everglades. The Frenchman, Mousier Jean Chevelier, was standing with Richard Harden, Tom Brewer, and Bill House, who had come to the gathering with his daddy, DD."

"Mysyoo Hairden, you tellink me thees sheety leetle toy ees a boot to carry allygaitoor?" Chevelier laughed so hard his thin body floated back into Bill House, who just shook his head and nudged him forward again. "Ah you Amerrycain even love puttink valyoobul title on sheet." He laughed again, "You not taking sheet, you aire having bowel movingment." He laughed and pointed at Totch's little home-made boat, "I can seeing Napollyeine crossing Rhine to keek bowel movingment out of dem foking Chermans." He laughed again.

Richard Harden's voice was hard when he answered. "Jean, you ain't never knowed much about this swamp and the way us folks earned our bread. I've seen men, not squawkin little Frogs like you, but real wilderness men that took ever dang thing they needed from the swamp, brung in a hunert or more gator-belly flats all rolled up in boats just as small as this'n here."

"Well Mysyoo Hairden," Jean Chevelier's voice was, according to Edgar, still as weak and scratchy as it was during his final days on Possum Key, "while your people foking goddamm swamp injun and Negro slaves, I dining weeth French royalty. I come on boat to America to fine a great treasure bury on Possum Key by French pirate so I can help my King when I go home. Meestaire Watson stop by an say he geeve me money to go home to France eef I geeve him quit-claim to Possum Key. I tell heem, good, you come in week an I be ready to go home." The emaciated old Frenchman looked like a Blue-Tick hound that had been kicked by his master after chasing a coon up a tree. "My sheety luck stay weeth me, because I die before Meestaire Watson ees able come back. He take ever goddamm ting in my pocket, eencluding dollairs he geeve me, but I not caring, for what I gone need dollairs een grave? He bury me on my island, so now I have nice place to rest unteel God fine place for me in Heaven."

"While you was livin like a goldang hermit and was just a'wastin away," Richard Harden said loudly, "my boy John Owen and my young daughter Liza, brung you food pert'near ever day and took care of you as if you was kin. They didn't regret doin it juss 'cause you had earlier promised to sign over to them your rights to Possum Key. Nossir, it was 'cause they was heartbroke to learn, after you had died in that shack, that it belonged to Edgar Watson. You sold it to a man that you always said you hated."

"Eet was time for me to go home. Your childs, or maybee you, gone geeve me dollaires to get place on boot to France? Sheet no you not, I nevaire see you once weeth cash dollaires, only small coin in you steenky overalls."

Jean began waving his arms, just as Ted and Edgar said he often had a habit of doing when things did not go his way. "Merci, crazee when alive, an now when dead, I see Mysyoo Hairden is same crazee fool."

Five minutes after Jean Chevelier had floated through the rear door, Edgar Watson came through the same one. Ted said quietly, "Didn't know if he'd come back or not."

Ted Smallwood, DD House, and Erskine Thompson were still sitting at the table beside the passageway. I had seen a nice big desk chair on rollers in the Post Office, so I dragged it out to sit in. That porcelain stove-top was sure not a good place for a man with a physical deformity like mine—noassatol...born with it.

Edgar abruptly stopped when he got to the open archway that entered the west wing. He was standing at the same place he had during the first visit, but now there were two different people sitting at the table with Ted.

His eyes reminded me of the eyes of a Bengal Tiger I once saw at the Crandon Park Zoo on Key Biscayne before they kicked those animals out in 1981 to make room for the animals that live on the Key now. I had docked Floating Homestead at Crandon Park Marina, and took a taxicab to the zoo.

As I stood looking at the magnificent tiger, a boy about nine or ten years old walked up. I noticed that he had a small brown bag, but didn't have a clue what was in it until he threw a tiny coconut at the tiger. I had noticed them earlier lying on the ground beneath a coconut palm. "Hey," he yelled, "here's a few more for your lunch." He began laughing as he threw one after another from the bag as he tried to hit the tiger's head. I grabbed his arm and wrenched the bag from his grip.

"What in the hell do you think you're doing, you disgusting little freak?" I was still holding his arm as a woman the size of a small refrigerator came running—at as good a pace as you would expect a refrigerator to run.

"What are you doing to my son, you big ape."

"Nothing," I answered, "compared to what the police will do when I call them." I glared at the extremely fat 40ish bleach-blonde as I shoved him at her. "I'm heading to the office now to give them both of your descriptions so I suggest you get outa here right now while you can." I turned and headed straight toward the only building that resembled an office. When I got there I looked back and watched as she literally dragged the mean little cretin toward the parking lot. Moments later she roared out in a huge black Lincoln. I've often fantasized about watching as that tiger pulled the bars back and jumped the little brat. Later on my mind modified the dream to make his mother come running, only to be torn to shreds too.

When I looked up into Edgar's black pupils he was staring at DD House like that tiger stared at the boy. As if a switch had been thrown, Edgar's eyes mellowed and he spoke very softly without a hint of sarcasm, "Hello Mister House, howdy Erskine, really good to see you again. Ted, you holdin court, or can anyone join you fellers?"

"Ain't no more chairs," Ted said, "but yer welcome to join in on the conversation."

Edgar just stood there a moment, kind of like some evil entity looming over DD House.

I had read Peter Matthiessen's excellent book, Shadow Country, which told the entire story concerning the series of events leading up to Mister Watson's death. DD House was the accepted leader of the armed mob waiting down below the trading post when Edgar returned with Leslie Cox's hat. Edgar had earlier been accused of killing some of his hired help rather than pay them. Their bodies had been found, but no direct evidence had been located to link Edgar to the crime. He had told his accusers that it was his crazy foreman, Leslie Cox, who had killed them, and he was going to his plantation at Chatham Bend, and either bring Leslie in or kill him and bring his body.

After running his motor-launch up on the beach, he confronted the armed citizens of Chokoloskee. "Here," he said as he held up Leslie's hat in one hand, his other holding the double-barreled shotgun that was always with him, "it's Cox's hat and," he shoved his finger up through a hole, "this is the hole my bullet made when he refused to come back here with me."

DD House then told Watson, "It might be a good idea to hand over your weapons, Edgar."

Watson growled, "Nossir, Mister House, that ain't a good idea atol."

A moment later, DD's son, Bill House said, "You're under arrest."

Another man in the crowd of motley vigilantes, Isaac Yeomans added, "A citizen's arrest."

Edgar spit his contempt on the ground, "You boys are full of shit." He glared at the crowd, his dark black eyes scanning them all as though to memorize each man individually. "Y'all have a warrant?"

DD House told Edgar to lay his gun down by the count of three. Before any count was started, Edgar looked first at Henry Short, and then while still looking at the Negro, raised his barrels and pulled both triggers, knowing some of the buckshot would get DD House.

Before anyone saw the 12 gauge pellets rolling out the end of both barrels, guns began going of as if a grand celebration had begun, but unknown to any of them, the notorious Mister Watson was already dead—a bullet from Henry Short's rifle ended his tenure on Planet Earth.

I could see the tenseness taking hold of DD House with Mister Watson standing directly behind him. "Erskine," Edgar said in a soft gentlemanly voice, "I don't recall us talkin to one another much back then," he laughed, "Hell's belles, anyone workin with me had barely time to keep his kidneys n' colon flushed out. But when we did, I recall you bein one of the bright young men, and one I could trust. They was a lotta two-faced fellers back then, and I just wanted badly to tell you now, personal like, that I never figgered you was one o' them two-legged snakes."

He adjusted his hat and turned toward the east wing, "I'll see y'all after while." He paused briefly to look at the entrance to the Post Office, "I never woulda believed that you coulda built up such a nice trading post, Ted." He looked past DD House toward Mister Smallwood to say, "I reckon they knew what they were doing when them federal folks made you Postmaster." He didn't even look at DD House. Edgar just turned on his heel and walked casually into the east wing.

"I suppose," DD said, "Edgar still bears a big grudge against me for what happened down below that day."

"Well DD," Ted said, "you was the one that got everyone all riled up. If them shells in the double-barreled shotgun had been good, I reckon you and your boy, Bill, would have been so full of double-ought buckshot it woulda taken three men to carry each of your dead carcasses back up to town."

"I don't think so, Ted." DD House leaned forward, talking in a soft voice, "A split second before he yanked on them triggers, and I saw this with m'own eyes, Edgar glanced at where Nigger Short was standing all alone off to his left. I had raised Henry as if he was m'own child from back when he was nothing but just a small black whippersnapper. He had his 30.30 rifle up n' pointin straight at Edgar, and I knew right then that he wasn't gonna let anything happen to his pappy, which is what he always called me. That rifle o' his popped and Edgar spun around a bit and was lookin straight at me. He had a blood spot on his forehead where the bullet went in, but he was a strong minded man, so he pulled on them two triggers while they was a'pointin down, and that's when I saw that buckshot come runnin out o' both barrels. He dropped the gun, but was still on his feet when everyone began shootin at him. But I still to this day believe that Nigger Short kilt him with one shot."

"And that's exactly the way it happened." Edgar Watson had silently walked up the original middle section after looking through the east wing. Must have walked through the big door at the end of the east wing and then through the main door to the porch at the end of the original trading post. He was known to be a soft and stealthy man when alive, and now as a ghost he moved about in absolute silence. We learned later that he could also materialize and vanish at will. Doing that required intense control of the energy that surged through this new entity now in charge of the once living Edgar J. Watson.

"Before I got outa my boat I saw Henry working his way out beyond them tree limbs. I knew, even though me n' Henry had a good relationship, that he was gonna see to it that the man he'd always considered his pa, you DD, didn't get shot or maybe killed. He knew me well, so he figgered he'd only have this one chance to protect you. Henry always hit what he aimed at, and that day he was aiming at my forehead."

DD House's dark bushy eyebrows furrowed down but he remained silent and I figured he was running all that through his mind again. I looked up as Edgar removed his hat and used his other hand to ruffle through his dark red hair.

"If some of the people that I spent a lot of time locating," he looked so hard at DD that the man felt it and swiveled around a bit to look up at him, "show up here for this unexpected little cadaver reunion, then y'all will finally know what happened at my plantation down at Chatham Bend. I reckon some, especially you DD, are gonna be thunderstruck. Maybe after this you'll all be able to allow your energy to die down. Ha, that's an odd way to phrase it huh? Anyway, let the energy phase on out and then you folks can move on to Heaven or Hell." He looked down at DD with hard eyes but said nothing.

"If that's the case, Edgar," Ted said with a slight smile crossing his face, "where will you be heading?"

Edgar Watson smiled wide, "I already lived my Hell right here on this earth, Ted, and I'm enjoying myself so much that I can only assume that this is my Heaven." He looked at each of us before asking, "Any of you ever been on a jet airliner?" After the three men at the table shook their head no, he asked me, "How about you, Py."

"Nope, I'm pure chicken when it comes to flying in something that has the glide ratio of a huge boulder when the engines stop."

"Well," Watson now had a mischievous grin, "I got on a flight heading out to Oklahoma a while back. At least that's where I'd planned to go, but circumstances caused me to get off in Tampa. Later on I'll tell you all about it." He replaced his hat and strode away to look through the trading post a little more.

At that moment a huge loud explosion was instantly followed by several smaller ones. The men at the table all sorta jumped up in their chairs. Several in the east wing screamed and rushed into the center in a herd. Their heads swiveled as their panicky eyes darted back and forth. I noticed that Edgar just stopped and stood in one place puffing on his apparently immortal cigar. (It never got any smaller and was never lit—musta gone out and had been in his mouth when he died?)

Jean Chevelier rushed into the center and stopped next to Edgar. His eyes were wide with fear and his head swiveled to the back door and then the front door as though he expected the Gestapo to rush in.

"Settle down boys," Edgar calmly said in his soft controlled voice, "them celebrating locals are just setting off Independence Day fireworks and there'll be a lot more before this evening's over."

DD House spoke so softly that both Ted and Erskine had to lean forward. I was glad Ted asked him to repeat it, because even though my hearing's still pretty good, I couldn't make out what he'd said either. DD glanced at

Edgar, and feeling secure that he was far enough away that he wouldn't hear, DD repeated, "He's always been a big blow-hard, sayin he's gonna do this or go there or build this or buy that."

Ted leaned back and then sorta looked at DD over the top of his spectacles, "Seems t'me, Mister House, that he always did what he said he was gonna do."

"Hog wash," DD abruptly stood and moved to the end as far from Mister Watson as possible, and started a conversation with Jean Chevelier. I noticed a few minutes earlier that Jean had all of a sudden thrown both arms above his head and shook them as he stormed away from Richard Harden, Tom Brewer, and Bill House, DD's son. DD moved in with the three men and began to nod with his head toward the area that Edgar entered.

Ted noticed it too, and said, "He's never gonna admit that he instigated that confrontation with Edgar. If he woulda just let nature take her natural course, that disastrous event might not have ever happened, and Edgar would have lived out a full life as a very successful man." He looked at me as I was busy taking notes. "Py, you like a stack of flapjacks now n' then floating in a bath of syrup?"

"Yessir, Mister Smallwood, at least once a week." I patted my ample belly, "As you can easily see."

He chuckled, "Well, you got a good idea then where this came from." He patted his own bulging mid-section that was asking for a size larger overalls. "I reckon I've tried about every corn syrup made anywhere in these parts, and believe me when I say that Edgar's was the best by a mile. I wouldn't be surprised to learn that he carried five hundred gallons of his to Key West alone. And when that freighter began sailing in here regular, he always had a batch jugged up n' ready to go north to Tampa, and sometimes New Orleans too." Ted leaned back and looked like he was letting his thoughts drift back to the past. "Yessiree, by golly, I reckon Edgar mighta left his mark high on the tree if he'd been allowed to live another thirty years'r so. Makes me wonder if DD House made a bad blunder that day right down below this trading post."

I wheeled nearer the table so I wouldn't hafta talk too loud for Ted and Erskine to hear. "You think Edgar actually has some people coming here that will tell everyone what really did happen that day?"

"Wouldn't surprise me a bit if he does, Mister Py." Erskine leaned closer, "I never knowed Edgar to lie outright or even to stretch the truth a wee bit. He always just told it the way it was, and let folks take it or leave it. Warn't many other folks here back then what had any backbone, exceptin Mister Smallwood here," he nodded at Ted, "and Mister McKinney. We's all so busy stayin alive that we just never paid no mind how things was goin as long's we had enough grits n' flour to last another month. And then along comes this big red headed feller with enough confidence in hisself, it coulda been divided up amongst ever dern one of us n' he'd still have enough to carry him right on through all of his plans n' dreams." Erskine looked hard at me when he added, "And that's why so many was skeered to death of him. Some folks said that he was the antichrist. I heard it m'self, more'n once. They said it would be a good day when he was gone from this place." He leaned back in his chair and closed his eyes as his head shook slowly back and forth.

"I heard that myself on two occasions." Ted said. "I told those who were a bit leery of Edgar that he was simply a man with energy and ambition and they shouldn't begrudge him that, because we'd all benefit in the long run. Some of these men look in a mirror and see themselves as som'n that ain't there n' never could be. Then they see a man like Edgar who carries with him everything they've ever wanted to be. That's when they begin to look for ways to whittle him down to their sorry state, so they won't feel so poorly about themselves."

"Good Lord a'mighty." Edgar Watson's booming voice turned all heads in his direction. "Look there n' see what blowed in on a sorry south wind."

Everyone but me knew it was Green Waller. Later on I could recall reading about him in Peter's book, and his description fit him like mosquito repellent in the swamp. Horse-faced, bad skin, and gimpy.

"Green," Edgar said, "you're as sorry lookin a ghost as you was a live man. Shoulda fed your drunken ole carcass to m'hogs, and started to once. But big ole Hannah come a'runnin'. She was yellin loud for the whole darn world t'hear that she loved you and would leave if anything ever happened to you." Edgar's grin was wide, but Ted had already told me that a grin on Edgar's face was often just camouflage. "You runnin from the law," Edgar said through the grin, "or on a cruise to see what the world looks like now?"

"Ain't neither of them guesses right, Mister Watson. Ole Tant Jenkins tole me they was gonna be a git together here at Mister Smallwood's store. He said mebbe you'd be hanging around here."

"Well now, ain't you a witty ole bag o' bones, Green. It's sure a mighty big jump from hog thief to court jester." The grin on his face now had a sinister wrinkle. "I hear that every now n' then the cattlemen in Florida hang a cow thief before the law can get to the scene of the crime, so mebbe we'll have us a hanging after all."

"I felt bad Edgar, about lettin them hogs o' yourn out so's they could go into the syrup mash n' git all drunked up. Felt terrible when I seed that half et carcass what a panther jumped. I reckon we's even, cause the way you named thet young sow I broughtcha, Topsy, she musta give you lots of enjoyment. They's better'n dogs to provide a man companionship."

"Well, I reckon you're right Green, and I surely did enjoy her the whole time she was there, but I s'pose she never was really mine, was she?"

"Huh?" Green Waller's self-confidence was waning as his voice cracked. "Uh, er, uhmm, whatcha mean, Mister Watson?"

"T'my knowledge," Edgar said as a sly smile began crossing his face, "y'ain't never bought a hog in your life, so I always was curious who you stole ole Topsy from."

Without hesitation Waller blurted out nervously and a bit too loud, "DD House."

By the panic expression that crossed his face when he heard DD House's thunderous voice, he hadn't noticed that he was in the trading post.

"Why you sorry son of a rustler," DD's voice sounded like close thunder to Waller, "you stole one of my sows to carry down to Chatham to cover your own drunkenness." His hand slammed hard on the heavy wooden counter,

"Yes, by God, we just might have a hanging before this night's over."

"Uh, er, uh howdy, Mister House," Green Waller stammered, "Didn't see you sittin there."

"Nah," DD snorted like a mad bull, "I reckon you didn't see me, you no-account stinking hog thief."

Mister Smallwood turned his head and looked at DD for a moment, and then shook his head. "Ain't no reason," Ted said softly, "to start all this rehashing so long after those days."

DD turned from Green Waller to look hard at Ted Smallwood for a long moment. He finally said in a loud voice, "Reckon you have a point there, Ted, but I had no use for a thief then and still don't." He turned again to face Green Waller, "Green, did you ever come by anything during your lifetime that you didn't steal from some hard working family?"

"I worked hard m'self," Green said in a shaky voice, "up at Mister Edgar's plantation on Chatham Bend." He looked around at Richard Harden, Tom Brewer, and The Frenchman, Jean Chevelier. "And," his voice took on a firmer tone, "I ain't never one time stole a thing from him."

"Why you lyin sack o' shit." Edgar's voice sounded to Green like death coming for him a second time. Edgar Watson took a step toward Green while pulling back his long coat exposing the long-barreled pistol.

Green knew, or should have after nearly a hundred years, that Edgar couldn't shoot him, but he leapt up and ran straight toward the closed doors that led to the porch overlooking the bay.

He hit them at a dead run, but bounced off like an unsuccessful fleeing cat. He heard Edgar growl like a maniac. He quickly concentrated on his inner power source, and a moment before Edgar was near enough to grab him, Green Waller was glowing red as he got up and began flowing through the wooden doors.

"Ha, ha, ha," Edgar laughed until he was forced to bend over and support himself on his knees, "spooky ole scarecrow ain't changed a bit in all these years. Oh my God," he groaned as he tried to regain his breath, "I knew I could scare him, but I sure didn't know he'd try to go through the door without building up his power."

"Meestaire Watson," Jean Chevelier's voice had a comical tone, "I watch as theece scarecrow go through the door. Was a beeg dark stain near hees ass. Mysyoo, I theenk hue make heem sheet."

Everyone, including me, laughed so hard we were all gasping for breath a few minutes later. The Frenchman only smiled briefly as he looked from one man to the next.

A short time later Edgar walked toward us. "You fellas wanna hear about that airplane ride I took a while back?"

"I would," I said, "can't imagine how you pulled that one off."

"Yeah, I'm curious." DD House responded, and then Erskine Thompson nodded his head, "Sure."

Jean Chevelier was standing very close behind Mister Smallwood. His answer was what we expected.

"Mysyoos', a good bullsheet storeee ees always a time passeure en situashione like dis." He stepped away and returned with a 5 gallon lard can to sit on. "Even dead as doornail over hundred year I must now sit or fall. No strength...dese goddamm foking wet Everglade leef me broking old man."

"You Frogs were broke comin outa the shell." Edgar smiled when he said it, but we could all tell that he had no use for the Frenchman.

"Those Frogs weren't worth a shit over in France when Yanks and Englishmen were trying to keep the damn Nazis from takin their country away from 'em."

Everyone turned to see who was talking, but I already knew, because I was looking right at him, and his picture was all over the trading post.

Jean was the first person to speak. "An hue, Meestaire whoever you are, know all aboot that, eh?"

"Damn right I do, because I was right in the middle of it during World War Two."

"Gentlemen," I said, "this is Totch Brown."

Ted twisted around to look at the speaker. "Howdy, Totch, I never expected to see you here."

"Was floatin through the area and saw that your old tradin post was just a'glowin."

"That obvious, huh?"

"T'me it was, but I don't reckon livin folks could see the glow."

"I hope not," I said, "because there would be so many people in here tryin t'figure out what it was, we'd all hafta go outside."

Totch looked hard at me, "Who're you?"

"I'm here to write an article about ghosts that folks say they've seen around this trading post. I'm starting to think it will be a book, though."

"I reckon," Ted Smallwood said, "there's been ghosts

around here for many years, what with the killin of Mister Watson and all the boys that was killed during them drug smuggling years."

"First time I ever been here."

Totch turned toward the voice, "And who're you?"

"Green Waller, I once worked for Captain Watson up yonder at his plantation on Chatham Bend."

"He uses the word work pretty damn freely for a fella that never let it get too close to him."

Totch turned his head, "Edgar Watson," he said as he held out his hand, "didn't reckon I'd ever get a chance to meet you."

"Ahh," the Frenchman groaned, "ees like hue meet a foking celebrity, eh? Thece man a celebrity like Jacque de Repare een Pairee."

Before anyone could speak, Edgar said, "Just another crazy Frog, Totch, don't pay any mind to the babblings of that fool." Edgar turned toward the Frenchman, "Jean, your mouth was always a few steps ahead of your brain. Jack the Ripper did his work in London, not Paris, you ignorant Frog."

"Craaazee eegnorant Frog, stupid foking Frog, Silleee old French man. Meestaire Watson, you more pain in ze asshole than when you is live." Jean Chevelier's voice had risen quickly to an almost screeching hysterical wail as his scrawny arms wavered above his head. He raised his right hand and gave Edgar a sign before storming back into the east wing.

"What's that thing with his hand mean," I asked, "touching his head with a finger then waving his hand toward you?"

"Means he thinks Edgar's crazy," Totch volunteered,

"I saw it many times in France during the war."

Richard Harden walked into the center of the store from where he had been talking to Tom Brewer, and Bill House. "What happened to get ole Jean all rattled?"

"Same damned thing that happened every time I got around that crazy old Frog." Edgar grinned, "Can't help but put the ole windbag down."

5

NEW ARRIVALS

A VOICE YELLED, "HEY Y'ALL, CAN ANYONE JOIN this party?" I looked toward the big door at the end of the central bay and saw a very short guy standing there with a grin on his face. I saw that everyone else was looking at him too.

He strutted toward us smiling, and stopped when he was close to Ted. "You're Mister Smallwood, aincha?"

"Yeah," Ted answered, "but I don't believe we've ever met."

"Pete Haines," the little guy stepped forward and held his hand out to Ted, "you quit running this store quite a while before I moved to Ochopee, but I come out here quite a few times back when your daughter Thelma was running it. "

Ted reluctantly took the little guy's hand and shook it, then looked around, "Any of you fellers recognize him?"

One by one the others said, "No."

"I remember you now," I said. "I met a gal out at the Golden Lion one afternoon when I was out there having lunch. That was when I came here in the eighties to write a piece about the local stone crabbers. She talked me into going to bingo out in Ochopee, and you were callin the numbers."

"Yep, that was me."

"She said you were the Mayor of Ochopee, but she said it with a nice smile and her eyes closed while her eyebrows went up."

"Y'ever been out to Ochopee?"

"Rode out there with Jigs Brown one day to pick up Cecil at Jerry's Fun Bar. I saw that little Post Office on the way out n' asked him to stop on the way back so I could take a picture of it."

"Well then, you know how funny it sounded when m'friends introduced me to Yankees as the Mayor." Pete chuckled, "I don't think there was more'n a dozen people lived there back then."

Ted Smallwood sorta snorted, "That Post Office looks more like a community outhouse that a Post Office."

"Yeah," Pete said, and then laughed, "a one-holer."

"How long has Ochopee been a town?" I asked.

"Warn't hardly a thing there," Totch drawled, "until a few years later, when Raymond Wooten started selling airboat tours to tourists. That was back in fifty-three. Once he started catchin gators n' crocs, the tourists came to see 'em. Purdy soon he had all kinds of birds, n' animals too, so them Yankee tourists started comin in droves. Most folks up north had never seen a gator or a crocodile, or any wildlife outside a zoo where they was all in cages. Ray had t'start building more airboats, and fore long his place looked like a dern used car lot because they's so many Yankee folks stoppin there."

"Gitcherself a chair, Pete," Edgar said, "I was just gittin ready to tell these folks about a ride I took on a big jet liner."

Pete rolled a wooden barrel over and put an empty coke case on top, upside down to sit on. After getting the pillow off the yard lounge sitting right across from me, Pete said, "I'm a pilot, so I always like any story about flying. I flew P-38s during the war." He looked at Edgar, "And I hold the land, air, and water, crash record."

Edgar smiled and looked at Pete a moment before asking, "Howja manage that, Pete?"

I could tell immediately that he had taken a liking to Pete. I could understand that, because I already had too. He was a very affable guy and easy to like.

"Well, Mister Watson, I was flying in my little J-3 Cub one day, and just about the time I was getting near Tamiami Trail I heard the engine beginning to spit n' sputter. I was heading to Everglades City and was pretty damned low too. And just about the time I got near Tamiami Trail it dawned on me that I was oughta gas," Pete grinned at all of us before continuing, "didn't have a fuel gauge. *Oh hell*, I thought, and a second later I hit the boat that a car-hauler had tied up on the top of his rig.

Knocked the thing clean off and into the creek. I sorta bounced," Pete looked at us again, "those J-3s are light as a feather and float around like a kite. I kept the wings level and the nose up n' slid her tail skid into the sawgrass."

Edgar slapped his leg, "Land, sea, and air crash record. Heh, heh, heh," he laughed hard several times while pounding his leg, before turning toward Pete. "That when you died?"

"Oh hell no, probably only doing forty when I put her down. It was years later when I was killed. Went down out there in the bay when I was flying an old twin down to Marathon. Me n' a pal bought it a month earlier, and was gonna start taking out charters. We had just left the EC runway about a quarter hour earlier and was still climbing when all of a sudden both engines quit." Pete shook his head, "I lowered the nose a little and switched magnetos and tried to restart, but nothing worked. That damn plane had the glide ratio of an anvil, so next thing I knew we hit the water." He looked at Edgar now, "What's this about flying in a big jet airliner?"

"Well," Edgar said as he removed his hat and fanned his face with it, "Ain't nothin to it really, as long as you've learned how to build up your energy and know how to get inside and stay away from people. Because even invisible, they'll know som'ns not right if you bump into one of 'em."

Edgar's face broke into a grin before continuing, "First time I flew on one, I slipped in right at the tail end, and stayed away from the gal in uniform while she watched the door close and lock. The two seats right in front of the door were vacant, so I kinda floated around and sat down on the inside one so I could look out the window." He shook his head, "No more window seats for me, 'cause it seems t'me everyone wants to sit by one. Anyway, I'm looking out at the trucks whizzing along down on the highway, and goin past all them new stores in Naples, when suddenly I saw this huge lady movin past the edge of the seat next to me. I figured she was changin seats, so was on m'feet in a heartbeat. But as I moved past her she began screaming and yelling that som'n stepped on her foot, and as I moved over her humongous body she started screaming about a snake or som'n crawling across her."

"Damn!" Pete exclaimed.

"For cryin out loud," I said, all taken up in his story, "what the hell didja do?"

"Well, I took a chance that nobody was gonna sit by that big fat hysterical woman, so after she squeezed into that window seat I sat in the isle seat next to her. I could tell that the lady in uniform was really leery of Jumbo by the way she'd been looking at her. I figured that if they landed and made her get off, then I was gonna get off too, if I could that is, without causing any more problems. Jumbo settled down though as soon as that gal brought her a tray full of snacks and three bottles of soda pop. First stop was Tampa, so I got off with no problems. I had learned a lot and had no trouble atol getting on one later to get back home." Edgar put his hat back on, and then gave his head a little shake, "I ain't got any idea how them jet motors work, but one thing I do know is that nobody in my day woulda ever thought som'n that fast would be zooming across the sky."

A split second after the word sky was out of Edgar's mouth, another series of explosions began going off one after the other. I think everyone jumped again when the first one went off, but it was obvious to everyone that it was just some more of the fireworks going off to celebrate Independence Day.

"Ain't none of my witnesses gonna stop here with all this commotion," Edgar said, "so I'm gonna drift on down to my ole homestead anyway, and see what it looks like. Probably sit out by the water and watch the sun come up like I used to." He stood and adjusted his pistol and then pulled his long coat shut and buttoned it. "See y'all early next Saturday evening." Without looking at anyone Edgar quickly walked to the big door and just sorta oozed right on through it.

Ted Smallwood stood before speaking. "I don't like the idea of comin here on the Sabbath, so let's all meet here again next Saturday."

One by one they all followed Ted through the door without so much as a wave to me. Seemed kinda odd to me at the time, but later, after I was sitting on top of my boat with my huge cup full of coffee and watching all the distant, and not so distant, fireworks, I thought about it. *Them folks don't just live in a different time,* I thought, *they're also from a different time zone, kinda like Star Trek.* I laughed softly aloud and said, "More like a spooky scene from the Twilight Zone."

Sitting there looking west, a huge explosion sent something way up into the sky. Moments later another explosion, but farther up in the sky, sent out a shower of sparkling stars that turned into a huge flag. I watched spellbound as the United States flag materialized for a brief few moments, and then began falling. There must have been a hundred roman candles going off one after another as the flag fell apart. *Wow,* I thought, *somebody spent some serious bucks for that display. Still a lot of patriots around.*

6

TIME T'GO FISHIN

I WAS READY FOR A BREAK. I STILL DON'T KNOW squat about ghosts, but I reckon they were itching to get away too, and talk about all that had been said upstairs.

I slept soundly until almost noon. Since it was Sunday I was pretty certain Gary-Mac would be working on his boat. I saw that the tide was low, so I put on an old pair of canvas deck shoes and walked along the edge of the mangroves toward the McMillin property. Years earlier, when I came to Chokoloskee to write an article about the commercial mullet fishermen, I was so busy I didn't get time to look his boat over.

The next time I came here I spent a couple of hours on the boat watching Gary-Mac attending to maintenance, and then I wrote an article about his boat and all that's involved to be a full time stone crab & crawfish trapper. He set his crawfish traps in August in the Gulf of Mexico, and later in October he set his stone crab traps. The boat's a fifty-plus foot Marine Management that's one of the best commercial fiberglass hulls that I have ever seen. She's powered by a huge diesel engine that will lift a full load of several hundred crab traps or a full load of 300 or so crawfish traps. Once she's up on top and running at ¾ throttle, the boat can run across much shallower water than most, because it has a tunnel that was designed for the prop to be mostly up into it.

Today I came to the end of the mangroves and climbed over the oyster laden rocks at the western end of Viking Country. The property got that nick-name when Ray, the father, Gary and Duane, the two sons who decided to follow their father into the trapping business, all worked on or built their blue crab, stone crab, and crawfish traps on the property. Another son stayed in Minnesota to run the family farm, but visits with his family in Chokoloskee as often as the crops will allow.

As I walked toward Vikings Corey, the boat that was named after their son, Corey-Mac, I could see the huge engine hatch cover propped up. Just as I stopped on the west side of the U-shaped seawall into which the boat was backed at the end of each day, usually long after dark, Corey-Mac popped up out of the engine room. "Hey Corey," I said, "the old man gotcha doin maintenance while he sits in the shade sipping a rum and coke cocktail?"

"Yeah, Py, and I think I'm gonna join him." Corey's a very likable guy and always has a ready grin.

"More like a diesel fuel and bilge water cocktail." Gary-Mac's blonde hair and headband popped up between the engine and hatch stringer. After worming his way up through the space between his engine and the stringer, he stepped up on the diesel and then onto the deck. "Takin yerself a Chokoloskee holiday, Py?" Sweat had thoroughly soaked the homemade headband that he was seldom seen without while working. He picked up a rag and sat on the gunwale wiping his face while Corey-Mac bent down in front of the engine. Gary-Mac stepped over and looked down, "That wash-down pump belt need changing?"

"Nope," Corey-Mac replied, "just a bit loose, so I tightened it up."

Gary-Mac returned to the gunwale as his son climbed out. "I reckon she'll be okay till the belt stretches again; probably oughta put a new one on then, dad."

I watched as they lowered the engine box, and could see that it was a heavy one. "You'll never forget the day you let that sucker come down on your foot."

Gary-Mac grinned as he returned to the gunwale. "I almost did, one day. I was coming back from Marathon alone, and it was rougher'n hell, so I slowed down to see what was making noise in the engine room. Laid the cover against the gunnel and leaned down to listen. A five gallon oil can had busted loose and was hitting the corner of the engine. Fished it out with the gaff easy enough, because it was less than half full. The boat had wallowed around a bit, and was really bucking about the time I was lowering that cover. Felt like the boat jumped about three feet outa the darn water, and the hatch was jerked right outa my hand." He held up his hand with the thumb and forefinger about a pencil-width apart. "Missed m'foot by about that much." His grin was back, "These boots," he lifted one of his white rubber boots, "are about as much protection as a sock."

"Want a bottle of water, Py?"

"Yeah, thanks. I walked around, since the tide is out, and did not want anything in my hands but my gig."

"See any crawfish?" Corey asked, and then passed me the bottle of water his dad had tossed him.

After half the water went down my throat, I answered. "No, not even a short."

"If you're hurtin for fresh seafood," Gary-Mac said, "we're taking daddy and four of his friends from up in Minnesota out for a few hours of fishing tomorrow, and you're welcome to come along."

"Hot damn, yeah man, what do I bring except my pole, and what time should I be here?"

"Seven-thirty in the morning, and don't bring a thing. I have a good assortment of gear, and daddy's bringing a box of food and a coupla cases of sodas."

Corey-Mac added, "And there's also five cases of my favorite drink down in the front."

"Probably," I said, "the same thing you drank gallons of when you was about ten, and I first metcha."

"Yep, water's still the best drink on earth, especially when it's a hot day out on the water."

Gary-Mac took us to a new wreck he'd found with his electronics and had marked with his GPS. He got the boat anchored so it floated back across the wreck with the tide, and had Corey-Mac snug up the anchor when he hollered, to put us in a good fishing spot near the wreck.

I could always tell whenever I was with real, no-bull-crap fishermen by just watching them work. Ray McMillin moved around on the boat getting his gear like he was practicing to go on Dancing with the Stars. While we were all getting our poles and a live fish out of the baitwell, Ray had already chummed the water a bit and was lowering his line down.

Corey and Gary helped get the Minnesota guys all set up and their lines going down before they each grabbed a pole. Before Gary and Corey got their lines in the water Ray was already pulling a fifteen pound red grouper over the gunnel. He tossed it in the ice, and with another small live bait fish on the hook, he sent the line back down.

Everyone I had ever talked to or interviewed said that Gary-Mac was the best captain to go offshore fishing with, but he's retired now and only takes family and friends out now and then. His son, Corey-Mac is the best backwater guide to hire if you want some great back country fishing. His boat is a 24′ beauty with a huge outboard engine that'll push it 60 MPH...or more? All of his gear is top of the line to insure a good trip for whoever hires him.

There are advertisements for guides all over the area, but not many grew up chasing fish through and across the many unseen oyster bars that run along the inside of the barrier islands—better known as the Ten Thousand Islands. Those oyster bars stretch along the coast from west of Everglades City almost to Flamingo State Park.

Many wannabe 'boat captains' have donated all or the

Biggest part of the bottom of their boat and often the lower unit of the expensive outboard engine to the Bar-Search-Program............*See-if-you-can-find-an-oyster-bar.*

At times, usually during the winter months, Gary and Corey are both difficult to book for a charter, but it's always worth the wait if you want to do some serious fishing. Call the number below, and if they're busy, leave a number and someone will call you back. 239-695-4540

We hit the dock that day with enough fish to keep all eight of us eating freshly caught fish for quite a while.

Gary, Ray, and a couple of the Minnesota guys loaded the ice box full of fish onto the back of Gary's truck. The four guys headed to their motel room to get ready to have dinner with their wives. They were leaving early the following morning, so Gary told them he'd have their fish fileted and packed in ice in their box. "I'll bring the box to you at the motel, just give me a call after dinner."

Ray went with Gary to clean and filet the fish. I stayed with Corey to help clean up the boat and wash everything before putting it away.

Once the boat was clean and everything put away and locked up, Corey and I walked over to where his dad and grandpa were standing at the filleting station. "Go get cleaned up, grandpa, and I'll help daddy finish these fish." Corey pulled his razor-sharp knife from its sheath and began skinning the fish after Gary fileted them.

I've never been good at fileting or skinning, so I sat on the edge of the concrete floor of their huge chickee that sat next to the seawall. Corey's cell phone rang, so he wiped his hands and answered it.

After a couple of minutes, Corey returned the phone to

its clip on his belt and turned to me. "Py, I'm taking a guy out fishing for a couple hours, day after tomorrow. He's been fishing with me for several years and I know he won't mind you coming along if y'want to."

"Yessiree," I answered, "what should I bring and where should I be at what time?"

Gary turned and smiled, "Sure takes you a helluva long time t'make up your mind, don't it, Py."

I arrived at the boat ramp that's between Ray's stilt house and the chickee, about fifteen minutes after the sun began shoving the shadows aside. I had waited until I could easily see where I was walking then cut through the mangroves on the trail that local kids probably used a hundred years ago.

Walking past Corey's house I spotted his boat sitting on the trailer and hooked to his truck. There were lights on inside so I knew he'd be heading over any minute. I turned at Lynn and Gary's stilt house expecting Sam and Putt-Putt, their two Jack Russells, to charge me, but they musta still been upstairs asleep.

A car pulled in just as I got to the picnic table next to the chickee. By the time the guy parked over beside Gary's diesel fuel tank, Corey pulled in. After backing into the ramp, Corey got out and put Bandit, his Jack Russell puppy, up onto the deck. She sat there as though she was the deciding factor in getting the boat launched properly. She's such a smart little gal that she just might have barked if he didn't do it right.

Ten minutes later we were flying (not really—I think the bottom touched the water occasionally) along between some of the famous Ten Thousand Islands. (That's not slang for a bunch of islands—there are probably more than that) The tide was high enough that hitting an oyster bar was not a worry because all that was in the water was a little of the lower unit that held the propeller.

As we wove our way through the islands, Bandit held her position on the bow. She was the replacement for his Jack Russell that was stolen before I arrived in Floating Homestead. Smart as he was, and from all I've heard about him, that dog was created to be Corey-Mac's partner and pal. Bandit stepped in as if she'd been created just for this job.

My first act as President For Life would be to bring back impaling for people like the one who stole Corey's best fishing pal.

The guy with us loved catching and eating speckled trout, so Corey stopped next to a pretty good sized island. "Try a small all white spoon out there." Corey pointed.

Thirty minutes later the fisherman had put three huge trout in the ice box and had turned loose seven or eight that I would have loved to toss into a hot skillet, but he called 'em pups and set 'em free.

"Feel free," the guy said, turning toward me before he made his first cast at the next stop, "to grab one o' those rigs and get a few of these big ones to take back to your boat."

"Thanks, but I'm clumsy as hell on small boats like this."

While reeling in a redfish that had a spot about three inches in diameter, he said, "I went over to the trading post yesterday during low tide with Buddy Baer in his golf cart. He lives in a small trailer on their property, and is an old Navy pal of Gary-Mac's."

"Yeah," I said, "I've met him. He's a nice fella and he's built some real nice yachts in his day."

Once we got that huge redfish on the ice, he continued. "Bud really likes that boat of yours and wanted me to see it. Reminded me of a canal boat I rented when I returned to Ireland last year to visit my family, but that boat o' yours makes 'em appear a wee bit shabby."

He only wanted to fish for a couple of hours, because he had company coming at noon. So after one more stop, where the ice got a few more trout that musta weighed three pounds each, we headed back to Viking Country.

Corey tied the boat against the seawall while he went to get his truck and trailer. I'd seen him load the boat before and knew he didn't want or need any help.

The concrete slab that the chickee was constructed on, sits about three feet high on compacted shell with a reinforced footer and wall all the way around. I sat on the edge in the shade as he loaded the boat.

Corey had backed the trailer into the water just far enough to let the bow ride up on the trailer just enough for the keel to fit into the rubber roller. Once he felt it roll easily forward enough for him to be certain it was exactly where he wanted it, Corey hit the throttle just enough to push the boat forward. When he was sure everything was lined up he revved the engine a bit and the boat slid forward right into the padded vee on the welded steel post at the front of the trailer. After pressing the button that lifts the huge outboard up out of the water, he climbed down and secured the boat with a safety chain to a stainless steel eye-bolt protruding from the bow.

Corey pulled around to the fish processing area and parked. The fisherman pulled in right behind him, and before I walked around they already had the iced box of fish out. "We only hafta gut 'em Corey," the guy said, "because right after lunch I'll be on my way back to Lauderdale, and I'm baking them all tonight for a party at our place."

"I'll pack 'em in there," I offered, "if y'all want."

"Thanks, Py," the guy said, "I appreciate that."

Corey said, "I brought another box of ice, Py. It's under that blue tarp in the bed of the truck."

By the time I got the small box of ice out, there were already two gutted trout. I put ice in the gut cavity of each fish and packed 'em head to tail with the gut down then added ice and packed the top layer.

While cleaning his hands the guy said, "Ain't the first time you've done that."

I looked up and grinned, "Nope, and I watched you out there. Easy to see this wasn't your first fishing trip."

"You're right, been fishing since I was a kid in Ireland. Rather fish than do anything else, but the 'do anything else' brings in enough money to let me do what I love now n' then."

"I believe the proverb that states 'the hours spent fishing is not deducted from your allotted time on earth' is correct."

"I believe it's correct too, Py. Gotta run now." He waved as he pulled out of Viking Country.

Corey said, "Theresa and the girls are shopping this morning Py, so hop in, and after I drop off the boat, I'll treat you to lunch at Orlo's."

"Never turned down a free meal in m'life, Corey, especially at Triad."

Fifteen minutes later we pulled into Triad Seafood and saw that Orlo was sitting at one of the picnic tables in the breezeway under the roof. He waved as we got out. "I've got a special today for poor local fishermen and other poverty-stricken island dwellers."

Corey said, "I'm earning a dollar a day customary pay, so it wouldn't feel right taking a handout."

"Well, okay then." Orlo grinned wide, "Them damn crawfish heads're getting pretty ripe anyway."

We sat at the table and a moment later one of his waitresses brought us a menu. While we looked through it, Orlo said, "My boy created the best shrimp gumbo that I reckon I've ever had, and a buncha folks already agree with me."

"He's a really good cook," Corey said, "but I brought a hankering appetite for fried fish fingers and some conch fritters."

After ordering, Orlo asked if we'd heard about the 90 year old woman that was attacked by a gator.

"No," I answered.

"Yeah," Corey said, "but I never heard any details."

"It was Jim Webb's mama," Orlo said. "Py," he turned to me, "he's the owner of the hardware in Everglades City where I sentcha to get that lock for your bicycle. Her house is next to the canal right out on highway 29 in Copeland."

"That's straight on across Tamiami Trail when y'leave here, ain't it"

"Yeah Py, about two miles beyond the Trail. She was

out in her yard doin som'n, tending her flowers probably. About then an eight foot gator came up and chomped down on her leg. I first heard it was her hand, but the paper says she lost part of her leg. Dwain Daniels was driving by and saw Missus Webb being pulled into the water. Dwain has known her all his life. She was fightin, so the gator had released her by the time Daniels got there, but he was still able to shoot at it. He said him and her son Jim Webb, who happened to be driving by, carried her up the yard, and then called 911. A chopper showed up pretty quick and took her to Lee Memorial Hospital. On account of her age they didn't think she'd make it, but she's doing pretty good right now."

Corey just shook his head, "Damn! Walkin around in your own yard and get attacked by a gator."

Orlo said, "You wouldn't know anything about the beer worms lady, Py," he turned to Corey, "but you probably heard about her from your dad."

"Yeah, she sold beer and bait out in Ochopee, and a gator bit off her hand."

"Yep!" Orlo turned toward me. "Her real name was Clara McKay, and she was half Cherokee. She moved from Miami to Ochopee in the 50s with her husband and lived there about forty years. Her husband died, so she began selling bait, beer, and some sundry items in a little store they'd put together. She made herself a sign that just had beer worms on it with no 'and' between, and it became her trademark. The beerworms lady. In 91 a seven foot gator snapped off her arm while she was dipping water out of the canal, right down below her beer worms sign. A few years later she went to a Naples Nursing Home. Clara was way up in her eighties when she died, just before Christmas in 96. I remember, because she died the same day an old friend of mine was released from prison. Everyone out there called her Hokie, but the local Indians gave her a name in their language, Tough Old Woman." He stood up, "I gotta get back t'work now. See y'all later." He nodded at the food his waitress was placing on the table, "Bony ape tits."

We both had a piece of Triad's rich key lime pie after stuffing ourselves. In my case overstuffing with a second bowl of shrimp gumbo and a basket of conch fritters.

While we were waddling toward the truck, Orlo yelled, "Try the toes next time, Corey."

"Didn't know that fish had toes, Orlo."

"Then y'ain't been payin attention to the ones y'been catchin, junior."

Corey dropped me off at the path leading through the swamp to Floating Homestead. After thanking him for lunch and the ride back to my boat, I walked around the deck to check everything. The previous day, just after dawn, I had heard noise coming from the bow area, so I climbed out of bed and slipped on the brand new, still-in-the-package, camo pajama-bottoms that I bought at the thrift store in Everglades City for fifty cents. Looking forward I could see through the wheel-house window that two young boys were fishing off the bow. I checked to be sure the correct CD was in the player and that the volume was set on low then unlatched the exit hatch. They were so absorbed in watching their lines that they never heard me until I lowered the hatch back against the handrail.

"**What are you kids doing on my boat**?" I growled loudly. They looked about twelve years old.

"We're juss fishin, mister."

Looking at their clothes, which was shorts only and no shoes, plus they were both the color of a gumbo-limbo tree, I figured they were locals. I was careful what I said, because it was not a time to make enemies among the local folks or their kids.

"This is my home, boys, and I can't have anyone coming on board unless I invite them." I had the small remote in my hand behind my leg. From constant practice I knew which buttons to press, so while looking hard at the boys, I pressed PLAY. Only a moment later the low growls of a Rottweiler echoed from below.

I had recorded the CD with help from a Key West friend who had trained his two Rottweilers to perform one of the best acts down at Mallory Square every evening during the season. As they did each choreographed stunt, he gave them a shot of water from a gin bottle. They shook their massive heads after downing the shot and then emitted a loud, 'Phuuuuuuu' through their flapping lips.

By the time the two huge dogs had performed all of their stunts, and the gin bottle was empty, they wobbled around inside the small ring like two drunks looking for the way home. The plastic loop held by their trainer, which they were supposed to leap through, was grabbed by Bonnie who was immediately joined by Clyde as he chomped down on the other side. Together they wobbled around the ring, stumbling back and forth like one drunk telling the other which was the correct way home, all the time growling softly at one another. Bonnie would growl and pull on the loop to indicate that she knew which way to go. Clyde would answer with a growl and pull her back in the direction he thought was right. They finally agreed and stepped over the ring to begin their wobble-walk home.

After only a few staggering steps both dogs ran back to leap nimbly over the ring. After giving the loop to my friend, he put a plastic collection bowl attached to a wooden shaft, into each dog's mouth and they began working the crowd for donations.

If donations weren't forthcoming as well as my friend felt they should, he would speak into his mic, "Aw, c'mon folks, Bonny and Clyde don't wanna go back into bank robbing just t'get a bite to eat." That was the two dog's clue. They immediately got up on their rear legs and began walking through the crowd while emitting a broken-hearted whine, all the while holding the stick and bowl level.

They only had two minutes to coax donations from the deadbeats before the entire crowd headed toward another evening act. Before the act began tall thin donation bowls were screwed into place atop the short steel posts that held the ring together. My friend told me that on a good night, they did three shows and would go home with over three hundred dollars, and on a slow night they still made enough to cover expenses and still have a little dog food money, and some fun money too.

I let Bonnie and Clyde's growling from below go on for a few seconds before pushing the PAUSE button. I then turned and said, "Easy now, Hannibal, they're just boys fishing."

The tall boy was straining to see down the stairway. I had a professional outfit put sun-shield on the front tempered glass window, which was the only window, and it prevented someone from seeing inside, except at night if there was a light on inside. All of the portholes were small enough that a person could see very little even with his eye almost on the glass, or screen if they were open.

The boy trying to see the dog leaned down like he was gonna try to look through the window, which wouldn't have allowed him to see inside anyway. So I yelled, "Son, if Hannibal sees you looking through that window I might not be able to stop him from running up these stairs." I pressed the PLAY button again, and bumped up the sound, and they sounded like a pair of killers ready to tear something or someone apart. In reality they were as lovable as any dogs could possibly be.

After hitting STOP, I watched as both boys leaped to the dock and grabbed their bicycles. Moments later they were pumping toward the path through the mangroves.

I pulled the hatch cover to me, but before heading back down, I stopped and looked up at the rear door of the trading post. *I'm beginning to have second thoughts about this ghost project. If I hadn't seen them ooze right through that darn door myself I wouldn't believe anyone who told me they saw ghosts doing what I've seen. And I don't what to think about that visit from Robert the Doll.*

I just shook my head and headed down. *Might as well get those notes up to date.* After securing the hatch I sat at my desk and opened the ledger with my notes. I hadn't updated the notes for three days, so there was a bunch of big Post-A-Note sheets glued to four pages. I don't make a big show of taking notes, even though they all know I am. I jot som'n down and glue it to the rear of the stack, and then try to figure it all out when I get back to my desk.

I usually update the ledger as soon as I get back here, or if I'm tired, then the very first the next morning. I haven't been feeling good lately, which I attribute to age, but I'm going to my cardiologist to have my bilge pump checked when I get back to Key West. Anyway, that's why I've let the notes accumulate these past three days.

Took a couple of hours to decipher all my scribbling notes, and get them all in the ledger. I fixed myself a cup of Chamomile tea and sat in the Captain's chair. My left arm had been aching, and I suddenly noticed that it felt fine, so I sipped the tea and tried to imagine what it must have been like living here a hundred years earlier.

Before Ted Smallwood built this trading post it must have been one helluva rough life for those pioneers. Mosquitos and no-see-ums were enough to drive a sane person nuts, they had to catch or kill everything they ate, and all summer they had to watch the sky for signs of a serious storm.

I finished my tea and on the way to the sink, I thought, *and just about the time everything was going pretty good, wham, the hurricane they all dreaded hit and killed a bunch and left the rest with damn near nothing. Most just scrounged up what they could and with little more than toughness and will power, started all over.*

I wasn't feeling much better, so I climbed into my bunk to rest a bit. Before opening Kick Ass again, I lay the book on my belly and thought about those early pioneers.

Tough folks barely describes them. Many people today have no idea how hard it was for those tough ancestors of ours to build this country for us to live in. Today the electric goes off for a short time and they almost have a meltdown. The satellite dish won't pick up one of the hundred channels and the kids have a shitfit while mom and dad polish off a bottle of booze.

I re-read one of Hiaasen's columns before laying the book aside and closing my eyes. I chuckled and opened my eyes then picked up the book to read the last few lines again.

> On March 26, startled Haulover beachgoers watched as one man pulled out a machine gun and shot another, while still a third drew his own pistol and popped off a few rounds. A bystander was shot and wounded as he walked his three children out of the park.
>
> Just another day at the beach. If the undertow doesn't get you, the sniper will.

I laid the book beside me and closed my eyes again. *Sometimes I think we're progressing into a nightmare era just as the Romans did.*

I must have been exhausted because I slept until an hour before dark. I felt good though, so I grabbed my rod and tackle box and headed up toward the bow.

The tide was just beginning to go out, so I put on a small silver spoon that had red feathers. On the third cast I reeled in a two pound speckled trout. *Easiest supper I've caught in a while.*

I noticed that the pain running down my left arm was back while I reeled in the trout. With one nice filet in the freezer, I breaded the other and started heating a skillet. I love grits, so I started a pan of chicken broth, diced some onion and garlic to add to it, and cut off a chunk of sharp cheddar.

Once the trout was browned on one side I flipped it and added the grits to the salted water, and then turned down the flame a little and watched to be sure the grits didn't boil over. Once the boil returned, I cut down the heat and retrieved one of the Key Limes that Mama Dot had given me when I rode over on my bike one day.

I sat in the Captain's chair admiring the sunset while eating a King's meal. I washed everything down with Key Limeade, made yesterday with fresh limes. After the last spoonful of grits, I thought, *we woulda won that damn Civil War if the corn crop hadn't failed. Once the grits n' corn likker run out, them boy's hearts juss wasn't in it any longer.*

While washing the dishes I noticed that my arm was still aching pretty bad, so I stretched out on the bunk and began reading a new book that I bought at the Thrift Store. I've always loved western novels, and this one was starting great. It was not a typical horse-poop and shootemup western, but rather a story about early Native Americans. The title was People of the Wolf, by a husband and wife team, W. Michael & Kathleen Gear. He was with the U.S. Department of the Interior and holds a master's degree in anthropology. Kathleen is a former state historian and archeologist for Wyoming.

I hadn't read a dozen pages before I realized that their chosen careers had helped make this book as authentic as any I had ever read—and I've read a lot of books.

I read until almost midnight, and the first thing I did the next morning was to open my laptop and go online. I

Googled them and learned that they had written quite a few books prior to the 1990 one I was reading, and have a string of books they've written since. *Boy*, I thought, *I'm gonna read every one if they're all as good as the one I started last night.* I ordered another one by going to Amazon.com and opening Used Books. It was a 1992 book titled People of the Earth, and I had it sent to my Key West P.O. box.

The pleasure of starting a great book was offset by the visit from an old acquaintance—if a bag of rags sewn together can be considered an old acquaintance.

Not long after I fell asleep, a slight noise, or maybe an intuition? Anyway it caused my eyes to suddenly pop open. Before I got my hand on the flashlight, those eerie red eyes were glowing and looking straight at me.

"You will die."

I finally located the switch and turned on the flashlight. There was Robert the Doll, once again sitting on my counter using the same tin flour can for a chair. His beady little eyes were glowing red as I swung my legs over the side and on the floor. "So will you if I can get to my gun before you vanish, you goddamned little voodoo freak."

Before I had time to move toward my gun, Robert was on his feet, something I had never seen him do. He leaped out through the screen of the open porthole as a puffy cloud and didn't disturb the screen at all. His squeaky voice as he oozed through the porthole sent chills up my spine…"You **will** die." He actually screamed the middle word.

I had to run my fingers across it to be sure, and there on the tips was that same ancient smelly residue.

I got a bottle of cold Dasani water out of the fridge and after squirting some pomegranate berry BIO in it—my favorite, I took 2 sleep aids. It was 2:00 AM when my eyes began getting heavy, so I stuck the Post-A-Note where I stopped reading and flipped off the light.

My left arm started hurting again the moment I hit the switch and my mind saw those glowing little demon eyes. I felt a slight pain throbbing in my chest. *That damn little bag of rags,* I thought, *is gonna cause me to have a damn heart attack, yet.* I slept well until after the sun came up. I laid there trying to recall the dream I had about Robert. All I could recall was him standing there in his silly little sailor suit watching as I went steadily deeper into quicksand.

I finally got a pot of coffee going and put two slices of raisin bread in the toaster. Watching the coffee perk, my mind returned to the dream. I carried the tray with the coffee and toast on it to the Captain's chair and climbed in. Before taking a sip, I thought, *there's no damn quicksand around here?* After a sip while chewing the toast, I thought, *IS THERE?*

The two Aleve I took before coffee had finally taken away the pain in my arm, so I sprayed on some CVS—50 sunscreen that I treat like my American Express Card...I never leave home without it...and climbed on my bike.

When I told Orlo a few days earlier that I wanted to go out to Blue Crab Joanie's Restaurant just east of Ochopee to say hello and have a soft shell blue crab sandwich, he told me that he was gonna be busy all day until late afternoon, and to take his truck and visit whoever I wanted to see.

So that's where I was peddling toward. I have a good bike in Key West that I store in a friend's garage, and I try to ride it every day I come into town to burn off a little fat, even though friends are constantly asking if I want to ride along to the grocery market or the coin laundry. That bike has seven forward gears and is almost effortless to pump.

This one, however, that I bought here in EC at the Thrift Store next to the Fire Department for ten bucks has no gears. And even though I oiled it well and it has good tires, it's a good workout to ride the four miles to Triad.

On top of the plastic saddlebags that were on it when I bought it, in which I carry a couple of tools and my cell phone, on the board where they're attached I strap on a small cooler. After getting across the causeway, I pulled into the parking area in front of the Oyster Bar. After leaning it against a power pole, I got out one of the six iced bottles of Dasani and squirted in some of that MIO water enhancer that I buy by the basketful. My favorite is Berry Pomegranate, and after finishing that one I pulled out another and gave it a healthy squirt before returning the MIO to the saddlebags.

Five minutes later I was peddling my lard ass toward Triad, where a no-effort-for-motion vehicle sat waiting for me to climb in and turn the key.

Orlo tossed me the key and said, "I'm busier'n a good looking Tom in a cat house, so go wherever y'want, but be careful with that gas pedal, because that old sucker'll do a mile in ten minutes."

"I'm used to just loping along," I said with a grin, "in Floating Homestead, but I'll try to get used to this bullet."

I'd met Joanie and her husband Carl many years earlier when I came to Everglades City to write a story about the sawfish that are plentiful in the local waters—or at least they were back then. What Carl didn't know about fishing these local waters, his friends did.

After Carl told me all he knew about the sawfish, he drove me to Chokoloskee and introduced me to Totch Brown. After explaining all he had learned about them in a lifetime of fishing and poaching alligators, Totch asked in his deep swamp drawl, "If y'wanna go out n' see a few o' them crazy lookin fish, m'brother Peg'll probably take y'out in his skiff n' locate a couple. And if y'charter him he ain't a'gonna charge y'near's much as them fancy boat fellers over in Everglades that don't know a eatin mullet from a danged bait mullet."

Back then I docked Floating Homestead behind Orlo's Fish House. He put me in a spot that wouldn't cause problems when his stone crab and crawfish boats came in at dusk to unload their catch.

I was up before dawn, and true to his word, Peg Brown pulled in and tied up the skiff.

I had never met Peg until Totch took me by Speedy Johnson's Fish House, that's just beyond Orlo's Triad, and introduced us. Totch knew he was there talking to Speedy that day about something, so we'd jumped in his truck and headed to Speedy's place. Fifteen minutes later me n' Totch were driving back down the street to Orlo's Fish House, now known as Triad Seafood.

Totch headed for Chokoloskee and I went down into my boat to get ready for the skiff trip the following morning.

Peg had told me that he likes to get going by sunup, and true to his word there he sat. So with my thermos of coffee, six bottles of water, and six peanut butter and jelly sandwiches in one bag and my camera in a smaller one, I climbed aboard.

That skiff turned out to be a full-bore speedboat. We were doing about fifty miles an hour right across the bay towards Chokoloskee. We went past Viking Country and east through the bay. Even though it was high tide I could tell that we were running past shallow areas that would be exposed soon after the tide changed. I could see that Peg was very intently watching the water and he would occasionally make very slight changes in direction, so I figured that we were in narrow channels as we moved along closer to the edge of the mangroves.

Peg slowed down and we idled along the mangroves as he kept scanning the shallow water beside the boat. He turned into an opening in the mangroves so narrow that I thought he was gonna tie the boat to one of 'em. But after ducking down, a movement on his part that I instinctually mimicked—thankfully, we idled forward into a five acre mini-bay.

"Oughta be able t'gitcha one o' them saw-nose fish as they head back out with the tide." He turned to me, "You caint keep it, but I can hold it up so you can get a pitcher."

"Peg," I answered, "that'll be great."

He ran to the north edge of the bay and tied the boat to a mangrove limb. I could then see the small river that ran into the bay. I knew better than to ask a guy like Peg any questions, even though I had a bunch of 'em fermenting in my head, so I just silently watched.

"Them saw-nose," Peg finally said, "go up the river a ways to feed on small fish and clams. I'll get m'rigs and set 'em a'foatin out, and I reckon we'll have at least one."

I watched as he pulled a gunny sack out of the bow under the deck. His 'rigs' were amber glass Clorox bottles that must have been half a century old, because I hadn't seen one in years. He pulled a squid out of a tin can and put it on a barbless hook at the end of a short line attached to the bottle's finger hole. Peg put the last of the six bottles in the water and removed the rope from the mangrove limb.

After firing up the huge outboard motor we idled past all six of the slow moving bottles, and headed to the area we entered through. I wouldn't have been able to find that narrow opening with a GPS, but he stopped right beside it and tied up. "I gotta be sure all six git outa here without snagging." The first five went through easily, so we were both watching the last one when Peg said, "Hotdang, lookit there." His arm was outstretched and pointing at the first bottle through that was now about fifty yards distant. "Reckon we already got one," he paused a moment before turning to me grinning, "unless it's a dern otter or a turtle what was upstream a'huntin som'n t'eat."

He didn't want to mess around with it yet, so we idled forward watching the glass jug. He finally eased up to it so we could see what had gotten excited about a half rotten squid.

Peg maneuvered the jug until he could get a good hold on the two foot long sawfish bill. As deftly as those gals up in Apalachicola shuck oysters, Peg lifted the small fish into the skiff, held it tight with his legs, all the while holding that bill, which I learned later can be dangerous to anyone foolish enough to become careless. As he removed the hook with his free hand, I got my camera out and began shooting.

Once I told Peg that I had enough pictures to make the editor of the magazine jump-for-joy, he eased it back into the water while still holding its saw pointing upstream for a few minutes, so the water would flow through the gills.

After the sawfish swam off we retrieved four jugs and headed toward the sixth. I was looking at it when the jug was abruptly pulled under. "Holy shit," I yelled, "didja see that, Peg?"

"Yeah, I been watchin som'n nibbling on that squid. I reckon we's caught ourselves a bull shark." He turned the engine off, "Let's just sit here n' let that bugger wear out a bit."

"How about some black coffee," I said, "and a coupla peanut butter and jelly sandwiches?"

"Sounds like a right smart ahdear t'me."

Four sandwiches and half a jug of coffee later Peg fired up the engine and headed toward the jug, which was now about a hundred yards away. Peg idled down and got a pair of wire cutters from his tool box.

I watched as he finagled his gaff hook into the bottle's finger hole, and slowly lifted until we could see that it was a bull shark about five feet long. Peg cut the steel leader and we watched as the exhausted shark slowly swam away on top of the water.

"That hook'll be outa his mouth in no time atol." Peg then turned the bow west and hit the throttle.

As we retraced our course, I saw how close the oyster bars on both sides were. When the tide was out there would be no way a boat larger that his could get through between two bars such as the ones we were roaring past. I looked around for a post or a stick that he could have been using earlier to keep the boat from clipping a bar—nothing. My eyes were straining to see something—anything, that he had used. *Not a darn thing,* I thought, *that he coulda used.* I have always admired these swamp-cowboys, but it went way up after watching Peg Brown roar through these mine fields with nothing more than memory and a built in psychic GPS.

I pulled into Joanie's and parked under a shade tree. Only a clam-shell-toss from the truck was Carl's garage. He made a good living there until he died. Joanie's not a gal that drags her feet doin the woe-is-me thing. She's about my age and could have retired, but she likes having lots of people around her, and figured a restaurant would be a good way to battle the loneliness, and it would help keep Carl off her mind.

Before long she opened up with a good country band, and has been packing in the locals and tourists ever since. I've loved every kind of seafood that comes out of the world's oceans ever since I outgrew the nipple. I recall my dad, Elrod, coming home with a croaker sack full of clams when I was about three. He had made a grilling place out behind Ruanjeho beyond the dock where there was only sand. It was old airplane tire rim and a rack out of a chunk of stainless steel with holes in it. Me n' Lenin was all eyes as we watched them shuck those clams then sit 'em on top of the fire.

We were all shoveling them down as fast as we could as they sat them on top of that piece of stainless steel to cook for a minute. Lenin was a really smart boy—still is, but like me he's not a boy any longer. Anyway, after half of those clams were gone and was being 'converted' Lenin said, "Elrod, I'll betcha them clams would open right up and already be cooked if y'all just sit 'em on top o' that steel thing with the holes."

Elrod stopped shucking and looked hard at Lenin. A minute or so later them clams began opening just like in the movie, Ali Baba and the Forty Thieves, when they yelled 'Open Sesame' or som'n like that.

Elrod plucked one off the grill and severed the muscle then chewed that sucker a second before sending it right down to the 'conversion' chamber. All three of us just watched him until he said, "I'll be doggone, they even taste better." He looked at Lenin, "I woulda brought some home sooner but I been dreading all the work it takes to get them clams to the eatin point."

"Not anymore," Lenin said with a wide grin as he got another clam off the grill.

I walked in and waved, "Hi" to Joanie, who was behind the counter helping her waitress get everything ready.

"How ya been doin, Py," she yelled, "ain't seen ya in a while."

"Been livin the good life down in Key West."

"Ahhh," she rumbled, "Isle of Bones, I love that damn town."

"Me too, best damn place I ever lived."

"Y'ain't lived in many places then, have ya?"

I turned to see who was talking, and there was Floyd Brown sitting in a booth eating a huge pile of fried fish and sipping iced tea.

His smile was wide and sincere, so I knew he hadn't been drinking much, because he went right back to his plate of fish.

I first met Floyd a few years earlier at Larry Harmon's Chickee Bar. I met Larry at Tin City in Naples back in the 80s. He was born in the area and had gone to school in Everglades City with Lynn and Gary McMillin. I heard he had installed half of the septic tank systems in Everglades and Chokoloskee, and put his money into a section of land next to the Barron River Bridge just as you enter Everglades City.

He began building a resort on it during the last few years of the twentieth century. It was right on the water, so he also built a series of slips along the seawall he built right after purchasing the property.

Before he had many people permanently renting some of his modular homes, which he put atop poles so a storm or hurricane wouldn't ruin 'em, he began building a chickee bar. Tourists sat inside the screened in bar, but the rest of us sat under the huge cover attached to the bar, and put up with the mosquito or two (thousand) that occasionally wandered in every minute or so.

That first day I met Floyd Brown he said he was kin to Totch but I never heard him say how. Floyd's got more stories than a wandering snake charmer, and as far as I could learn, all or most are true. He told me about being left in the jungles of Colombia during the drug smuggling years as collateral until his friends returned with the rest of the money for the load they hauled home, and to get another load.

"I was left down there," Floyd said, "to insure that my

pals would return with the money and get another load."

I recall asking him what would have happened if they didn't return. He looked at me like I was a Yankee tourist wearing Bermuda shorts and wearing a long-bill hat with earflaps and sporting a nose painted white with pelican poop to keep from getting sunburnt.

"They'd of kilt me."

After a sip of his beer he said, "Them was the nicest darn people I ever been around. They kept bringing me young girls to impregnate because the lighter skinned a person from the jungle is the higher in their society they are." Floyd finished his beer and grinned, "In the three months it took for m'pals to get back I sure did my duty, because the last time I was down there, musta been at least more'n a hunert light-skinned kids runnin around that village. And by golly they all resembled me when I was a kid."

The waitress came by and Floyd ordered another beer. Floyd looked toward the bar and mumbled, "Aw shit."

Larry Harmon walked up and said, "Hi Py, see you already met Floyd." He leaned down toward Floyd, "You know the rules I set, Floyd, no talking to customers unless they try to talk to you, and then you only answer." Larry leaned a bit closer, "And no conversations, just an answer and then ignore 'em, got it?"

Larry's a tall muscular guy that never lets trouble get out of hand in his Chickee Bar. "Floyd's run off more customers," he said, "with his continuous chatter than any amount of mosquitos ever has." He turned to Floyd, "I've been counting your beers and the one I'm gonna have her bring you is number six and it's the last, okay?"

"Okay Larry, I understand whacha said, and I'll be in Monday to pay my bill."

"That'll be fine, Floyd." Larry turned to me before heading back inside to the bar, "As far as I know, Py, all of his stories are true, so y'might wanna write a column about him and his tribe of white Indians down in Colombia." He smiled then waved and headed back in.

I could tell by his speech that Floyd wasn't drunk, so I said, "That fish sure looks good but I have my mind and taste buds set on one of Joanie's softshell blue crab sandwich. What kind is it, though?"

Floyd glanced around to be sure nobody was nearby, then leaned over and said quietly, "Snook." He sat back up to get another piece, and while chewing he leaned over again, "Just order sea trout and kinda wink." He grinned and returned to his pile of 'trout'.

After eating the best softshell blue crab sandwich that I ever had, I waited until Joanie was caught up and her waitresses were handling everything, then went over and spoke to her. "When ya comin down to Key West to visit me, Joanie?"

"When I do," she said while walking over to lean down and rest her arms on the counter, "it'll be when I get this place set up so these girls can run it." I wish I'd had m'camera so I could get a shot of her sardonic grin as she added, "And that'll be the very same day that ice cold lemonade is handed out down in Hell."

We chatted a few minutes, and then I told her that I'd be back after the weekend for another sandwich.

She grinned, "Try the fried sea trout basket, Py, I'll make it myself and pile on the trout," she winked, "and fries. Where ya headin now?"

"Gonna ride over to Plantation," I said, "and look around. Always liked that place, because it reminded me of Fort Lauderdale back when it was a small town on the Intracoastal Waterway with ordinary folks livin along all those canals that ran in off the waterway."

"Since I last saw you," Joanie said, "I bought a place over there, and I love it. Here," she said and grabbed one of her menus, "I'll draw you a map so you can stop by one evening after I lock up here. The hours are on this menu." She turned it over and began sketching the route to her 'seaside mansion' as she referred to it.

I folded it and tucked it into my shirt pocket. "Thanks, Joanie." I waved and headed back to Orlo's 'rocket', "See ya soon for that 'sea trout' basket." I had to step aside as a dozen or so customers entered, and felt good that her place was busy during the off-season.

After cruising slowly around the streets of Plantation Isle, I headed back toward Orlo's Triad Seafood. *Man, I thought, Plantation has sure been upgraded since the last time I came over here.*

I felt guilty doing it, especially so soon after stuffing my gut with softshell crab, but I knew I was gonna need energy to peddle my big carcass back to Chokoloskee. I ordered a slice of their terrific Key Lime Pie.

Just as I wiped the plate with my finger, Orlo came out and said, "Let's toss that bike in the back of m'truck. I've gotta deliver six orders of fish fingers and conch fritters."

"Damn," I groaned, "if you woulda told me earlier I wouldn't have ordered that Key Lime Pie."

"And pigs lay eggs if y'feed 'em right." His crooked grin made me laugh.

We delivered the orders to the huge motorhome park across from the Post Office, and then headed to the path entrance so I could get to my boat.

"Pretty bad situation Lynn's in here. A lotta folks're gonna think her grandpa's trading post has closed up permanent, and the word'll spread. She might never be able to get it goin good again."

"Yeah," I answered, "what that guy from Sebring did was criminal and he damn sure oughta be jailed, but it'll never happen."

"Not with the legal system in this country." Orlo said as he shook his head, "He'll hire a buncha slick lawyers and she'll hafta hire lawyers too, and I know she ain't got money for that. So she'll hafta borrow it somewhere or he might wind up owning the property."

"That's what I think his plan was. Bankrupt her and he could then make her an offer for the property. It would be a nice chunk of land because it sits right next to the piece of property he already bought."

"Yeah," Orlo added, "he also bought the old motel and property on the other side of Mamie Drive that Lynn's daddy built."

All I did was shake my head.

After taking my shoes off, I climbed out. "Ain't much else she can do about it, but get a good lawyer and fight the bastard." I shut the door.

"Woulda been back in the seventies." Orlo said. "That jerk might never have made it back to Sebring."

I thanked him for the ride and began sloshing my way toward Floating Homestead pushing my bike.

By the time I got down below to my bunk, my left arm was really aching and a slight but frightening pain in my chest was worrying me. *My cardiologist in Key West told me to make an appointment for a stress test, but this job about ghosts came up and I never did.*

I recall thinking; *I might not make it back to Key West to take his dern test.*

After lying there a few minutes, the chest pain was not as bad and the left arm felt better. *Probably just got up too early and did a little too much today,* I thought, and got up to fix myself a cup of coffee.

I sat in the Captain's chair until a couple hours before dark. I knew that Sunday was going to be a stressful time for me if Edgar's witnesses showed up to substantiate his claim that he wasn't the one who killed those people who had been working at his plantation.

I made up my mind that I was gonna fish, read, and relax the next three days to be ready for another session with those Ghosts of Chokoloskee on Saturday night.

I was still pretty tired from all the running around on the previous day, so I spent all day Thursday doing som'n I had been putting off. Dumped everything out of my tacklebox and began tossing things in the trash can. My box is typical, rusty hooks, rubber worms stuck together, knife and pliers hard to open, lead all mixed together, a couple of lures that needed new treble hooks, more than a couple that had never caught a fish, so I removed the treble hooks and tossed all into the can—a bit difficult, since they'd been with me about 15 years. There was also a twenty dollar bill with rust all over it. I learned young that a bait shop will not give you live bait on the promise that you will bring the money next time. That wasn't the first time that I forgot to bring some money when I left Floating Homestead to go fishing somewhere that I couldn't get the boat in—but it was the last time I had to ask for credit to buy bait—live or otherwise.

By noon I had everything in the box organized, and all tools cleaned, sharp, and greased. I set it back against the wall above my three poles. After removing each one from the holder, I decided they looked fine, so all I did was add a little reel lubricating oil and replaced them.

I had some 100 mg Tramadol that my GP in Key West had prescribed for the strained back I received a month before heading toward Chokoloskee. I adequately showed all my macho old-man stupidity by removing the 12 Volt battery that supplies a couple of DC lights. It's a deep-cycle battery and much heavier than a regular battery. I then carried it duck-walk style to the stern where I somehow got it down into my dingy. Ten minutes later I hefted it up and onto the dock—ouch! That's when I got the strained back

I had several young friends moored out nearby that would have gladly come over in their dingy and done it for me. And they all knew I would drop off a bottle of their very favorite booze as a way of thanking them.

Old macho men don't do things like that though. We'd much rather show the younger generation how we can handle most anything, and then nurse our wounds and shove Preparation-H silver bullets up our ass until those flaming hemorrhoids go back up to where they came from.

What was another kind of pain altogether though, was after leaving the doctor's office, I thought, *I coulda given one of my young pals a bottle of booze to assist me for the next few years for what that doctor just charged me.* A young lady passed by and looked at me oddly, probably because I was mumbling, before moving away from me. I kept on mumbling while unlocking my bike. *And now I gotta go get a darn prescription for the pain pills that'll probably cost me more than another five bottles of booze.*

Knowing that I'd soon be leaving, I headed to the engine room to check everything out. After reading through the Maintenance Log and comparing the numbers on each engine's Hours-Used-Meter I realized everything was fine to head home on. The main engine and the little generator diesel were still running like they just came outa the box.

That guy who built the boat really knew what he was doing. Dual oil and fuel filters for the main engine were mounted on the fire-wall with stainless steel shielded flex lines. I could change oil and fuel filters in my church clothes—if I went to church. Both engines were mounted high enough for a pan to catch the old oil.

Forty minutes after entering the engine room, every task in the log had been checked off, and I was heading to the galley.

After fixing myself a fried Spam and egg sandwich, I put a glob of cottage cheese beside it, grabbed a two quart recycled milk bottle that I had filled with water and put a few squirts of MIO in. I climbed up into my Captain's chair for a late lunch. I say late even though it was only a little past noon, but since retiring to Key West I have fallen into a very sedentary lifestyle. At seven in the morning, noon, and five every evening my teeth begin to masticate, and if I don't shove food between them, I fear they might continue until some enamel was flaked off like a Native American making arrow heads.

I keep a fifteen-stick pack of Wrigley's EXTRA, Polar Ice flavor chewing gum in my pocket constantly, so when I can't be sitting in front of a plate of food on time, like a while earlier when I was in the engine room, my teeth won't have a meltdown and cause me to make my Key West dentist's fifty foot luxury yacht payment when I get back to the Island of Bones.

Half an hour later, I tossed the paper plate in the can and put the near empty water bottle back in the fridge. I had an afterthought and retrieved the plastic bottle. I finished the last of it, and poured almost two bottles of water in, and then put two long squirts of MIO in before shoving it back into the fridge.

My left arm had started aching again, and that pain in my chest had suddenly returned—not sharp, but enough to make me stretch out on the bunk and take it easy. I had already popped in a couple of Tramadol before I ate, so I didn't hafta wait long for the arm to stop, but the chest pain was still there. I read another column in Carl's Kick Ass, and then dozed off for a couple of hours.

Considering a dream I just had about reeling in a huge snook an omen, I grabbed my snook rod that already had a large plug attached and headed up the stairs.

I'm gonna pay more attention to my dreams from now on, because about 30 minutes later I was fileting an eight pound snook.

With several servings of snook packaged and in the freezer, I proceeded to fry two nice chunks for my dinner.

Feeling stuffed, I took a nice long walk. I stopped at Totch Brown's house, and while standing across the street I remembered how nice he kept it. *Still a pretty nice place*, I thought, *but not like it was when Totch and the Queen of the Everglades lived there.*

I'm sure Totch told me his wife's name, but he always referred to her as his Queen of the Everglades, so I guess my memory only remembers her as that, and dropped her real name into the recycle bin.

As I turned right and headed on down the street toward the kayak rental place, I thought, *sure hope a member of Totch's family buy's it and gets it back in shape.* My left arm began aching again, so I stopped at the corner across from the church and fished around in my shoulder bag. I took a big bite of the Snickers Bar, because I learned the hard way that you MUST eat som'n when you take a Tramadol. After swallowing the two pills with the candy, I washed it all down, and then tossed in the rest of the Snickers.

Before I got back to Totch's house the arm had stopped aching. My thoughts then were about my heart, *that ache in m'arm probably isn't heart related, otherwise the Tramadol wouldn't help, but the pain in my chest is another story. I'll call his office on Monday and make an appointment.*

I had decided to stay on the boat and rest on Friday, and was wondering what to fix for lunch, when Corey-Mac pulled alongside and beat on the hull. I went to the open porthole and asked him, "What's up?"

"Daddy smoked a batch of mullet and told me to run a few over here to you."

"Hang on, amigo, ahm a'comin right up."

Corey handed me up two gallon Ziploc bag with two huge butterflied mullet inside each. He then said "Here, Mama Dot gave these Key Limes to daddy an told him to give 'em to you." He handed me a small Ziploc with a dozen of the juiciest Key Limes I've ever had. She gets 'em right in her yard from a tree that she started with a seed.

"Thanks a bunch, Corey, this settles a problem. I was trying to figure out what was gonna be lunch and dinner."

He waved and headed back toward Viking Country at an idle.

Saturday began with a two-hour rain storm, which turned Viking Country into Lake Viking until afternoon when it would be dry crushed shell again. I could just about feel Floating Homestead luxuriating in a nice freshwater bath, because salt spray accumulates all over her whether or not the wind blows.

By the time I finished frying some bacon and heating leftover grits to put the three over-easy eggs on top of, my left arm was aching so bad that by the time I got two Tramadol washed down, breakfast was getting cold.

I put the arm in a sling I made the previous day, which made it ache less, and half-heartedly nibbled at the mess. As the pills took affect my appetite returned, and fifteen minutes later I placed a nearly spotless plate and fork into the sink. *Takes a lot to detour this old food converting machine.*

While washing the plate and fork, I chuckled when I thought about my buddy Eddie again, and his attitude about a 'food converting project' inside us of the food we eat.

I sat in the chair sipping coffee and looking west as it rained. *I'm pretty sure that this pain in my chest is related to som'n not right with my bilge pump.* I finished the coffee about the same time the rain stopped. Before getting up, I thought, *wonder if my cardiologist in Key West would send me a prescription for nitro to a pharmacy in Naples?* On the way to the galley, I had thought about it. *Hell no, he'd want me to go see a cardiologist first.*

After rinsing the cup I headed up the ladder. After I had closed the hatch and checked all around the boat, I unlocked the bike and rode to the primitive path through the mangroves. It was flooded, so I removed my deck shoes and placed 'em in the basket and walked the bike to the road. When I pulled into Viking Country I saw that Gary's boat was out and hoped he had taken a charter out fishing. Lynn's car was not in the drive, so I figured she was shopping. I rode back down the road and turned at the corner, then rode east to see if Mama Dot was home.

I was happy to see her sitting outside in her screened porch. "Hi, Mama Dot," I yelled as I put down the kick-stand.

"Good morning," she said as I entered, "you out doing your morning exercise?"

"Yep, been laying around in my boat for two days, and had to get outside. Nice rain, huh?"

"Yeah, and my trees and plants really love it. Look at the pear tree and how shiny the leaves are now."

"I'd sure love to have an avocado tree like that near where I moor the boat, but if there was," I laughed, "I'd soon be too big to get down the ladder."

"Yeah," she commented, "They're fattening, but they also have many good vitamins." She frowned and shook her head, "Them tourists in Key West would probably take 'em off the tree anyway before you could row your dingy in to get a couple."

"You're right there, because they go right into local people's yard and get whatever they see growing. If I could have only one tree though, it would be a Key Lime tree just like yours, because I eat a lot of fish and drink lots of lemonade."

"They're good for you, because they not only have a lot of vitamin C, but lots of other vitamins too."

"Yeah Mama Dot, there was a tree on city property when I first went down there years ago and moored the boat where I now live. A friend of mine told me it was full of Key Limes every season and local folks never took more than they needed at the moment. But when the tourists began coming down here during the summer too, those limes soon disappeared. He said they would come with baskets and strip it."

"I believe it," she said, "because there used to be lime trees on Chokoloskee and Everglades. Whoever owned the property never minded someone getting five or six limes, but people started stripping the trees at night to sell the limes. Homeowners who had lime, pear, and papaya trees soon began putting fences around their property." She shook her head and made a tsk sound, "In the old days nobody had any fences. We looked out for each other and saw to it that the kids behaved too."

We sat for about an hour as she told me about raising her two boys on a commercial fishing boat between here and Flamingo. "I came here from New York," she said, "when I was just a young girl. My husband was from here and knew all about fishing and boats. I was taught young how to cook, sew, can food for winter, and treat sick boys, since there were no doctors except in big cities, so we had a very good life living on the water."

Mama Dot said that she and her sister, Marjory, were thinking about writing a book about their life. I encouraged her to write it. "Because," I told her, "people who have never left the city have no idea how you could survive without all of the modern conveniences, and will buy it to learn how you did it."

I finished my glass of Key Limeade and stood, "Gotta get back to the boat while I still have enough energy to peddle the bike."

"Okay Py," she stood too, "I've got some strawberries to can." She watched as I got mounted then waved as I headed home. I waved back without looking, because it was all I could do to keep the bike moving ahead without wandering all across the road."

Actually I wanted to get back to the boat so I could lie down. The pain in my chest had returned.

By the time I was lying in bed, the pain was severe, so I concentrated on relaxing and thinking about some of the great fishing trips I had. Next thing I knew, my mind had dropped off into the twilight zone for a few hours rest, and it was getting dark. I lay there a moment and was relieved to know that the pain was gone. *I'll hafta remember that,* I thought as I lay there, *on the way back to Key West. If the chest pain gets bad, I'll stop and drop anchor if necessary, and rest until it lets up.*

Later, as I sat in my folding chair up on the roof of the boat, I heard a noise similar to the one made by the first bat returning to Carlsbad Caverns. When Lenin and I were young boys, Elrod and Hattie took us on a camping trip to New Mexico. We camped a few days in a bunch of areas in New Mexico, but the one I remember best was Carlsbad.

We all climbed on the bus and went out to the caverns an hour before daylight. A friend of Hattie's told her, "Be sure to take the bus out to the caverns and watch for the returning bats, millions of them, maybe billions? They get back just before daylight from feeding on mosquitos and any other bugs flying around in their territory. They power dive from way up in the sky, straight to their cave entrance by using a radar system built into their head, I reckon. You'll just hear a little poof, and then two poofs, and then the poofs from bats opening their wings just before they hit the ground to go back inside to their roost. It will be deafening for about fifteen minutes. By the time the last half million or so bats are going in, they look like a huge high tornado funneling into that cave. You guys won't be disappointed."

We weren't. It was the most spectacular natural nature display that I've ever seen.

I finally glanced up and there was Mister Smallwood, like a big fat bat, he was landing on the porch. "Evening, Mister Smallwood," I said just loud enough for him to hear, "I'll be right up.

Ted and I sat at the same table as before. He was in a reminiscent mood, so I silently listened as he talked about the early years when he arrived here to begin a family and his future.

At about ten o'clock we both turned toward the east wing. Without a sound the same bunch that had been here before came through the wide door and walked to where we sat.

It wasn't long before we all saw Edgar Watson walking toward us with three others following him. Two were the largest women I have ever seen. Not big fat blobs like we see today every time we drive past a fast food joint, or any other places where people eat or shop.

Nossir, these two gals were made out of bone n' solid muscle.

The third was a small petite dark girl that looked like a local Seminole Indian.

"Howdy gents," Edgar said around his still unlit cigar. His wide smile was the sincere mask of a man secure in his feelings of righteousness. "I had to use everything in my power to send a plea to these three ladies, but they all finally responded and met me today at my old plantation on Chatham Bend."

"That's great, Edgar," Ted Smallwood said, "but what do you expect to gain by this a hundred years after the fact?"

"Mister Smallwood, I backtracked m'self many times just to clear up untrue rumors about me. I know that I was not an easy man to get along with, but I never killed anyone that didn't need killin. Them scoundrels who I learned had taken great pleasure in slandering my good name, just so's they could be in the limelight for a brief moment to add luster to their boring monotonous lives, soon learned the error of their ways."

He pulled on the cigar as though it was lit, and then turned toward me. "Mister Lam, I hope you see the truth in the testimony these three ladies will have soon offered to give, as their attempt to clear my name as associated with these heinous crimes that I was unjustly accused of committing, and then subsequently executed by a local group of vigilantes, that under normal conditions would not be seen as fit to live amongst normal folks." Edgar turned, as did we all, when people—ghosts......began oozing through the rear door. "A vigilante group," his finger pointed, "led by that man comin toward us now, Mister DD House himself."

"You still babbling about that day?"

"Yeah," Edgar almost growled, "it was a special day, the one when you and your vigilantes ended my life, which was a life that I had planned to stretch out into about eighty years, so that my twilight years would have been spent right there at Chatham Bend watching my vegetables grow and syrup cane get tall and filled with sugar."

Edgar stood and stared so hard at DD House that he and those behind him stopped dead in their tracks.

"Mysyoo Watson," Jean Chevelier stepped out and moved forward, "Ow hue gone live so long when hue cut or shoot man's who making hue mad? Eh, hue tink people gone turn eyes away an letchew do whatever hue vant?"

Mister Watson stared hard at the Frenchman for a few moments, but then surprised everyone, including me, and pulled that long-barrel gun from its holster and screamed, "I shoulda done this a hundred years ago." Before Edgar could even make a move toward the Frenchman, Jean was through the door like an inflated balloon let go.

Everyone standing turned from the door as Edgar's boisterous laughter filled the trading post. Finally he straightened up after bending over to catch his breath. "I wasn't gonna do that, but then I thought, what the hell, I can't scare the old fart to death." His grin was infectious, plus nobody standing here had ever really liked the sour old Frenchman.

Most everyone started chuckling, even the three girls he'd brought with him. "I see you do that other time," The young Mikasuki said, "when I work for you. I like when you funny an not mad. I wish we still live."

"Me too," the big woman said.

"I never met the man that my sister," she nodded toward the slightly smaller woman, who was six feet tall, "worked for," this time she nodded at Edgar, "but I sure as Hell wish I was still alive."

There was a silent pause, and then a voice behind the crowd standing said, "Why Hell yes, we'd all like to still be alive."

"Didn't notice you coming in, Totch," I said.

"Didn't know whether or not to come on in when I saw how fast that scrawny old Frenchman took off."

"Edgar," Ted said, "played a little joke on Jean and he ran for his life." Ted laughed hard and everyone joined in.

"Totch," Edgar said, "I brought with me three ladies, one of which was murdered while she worked on my plantation at Chatham Bend, to shed light on the real, and I would think obvious, circumstances that occurred in my absence at Chatham."

"Well Edgar, I'm glad I stopped by, because I've heard or read all about that scene you got caught up in that day and I never felt like you killed them people. I reckon you mighta killed some guys along the way back then that needed killing, because those days were a lot different than now. Only a stupid man would kill off his help when there was little chance he's gonna find more to hire around here. I been down to Chatham when everything was still standing until these new morons they call rangers burned it all down, and that wasn't a place that a stupid man coulda put together."

"Well," DD House said caustically, "I ain't gonna stay here n' listen to a couple of girls and an injin tell some far out story about how somebody else did them killins when most everyone here knows damned good n' well thet you killed 'em."

"I never did believe it, DD," Ted said, "and I tole you so at the time, but you got it into your mind that Edgar done it, so you got that bunch of vigilantes together and guided 'em until the moment Henry fired to protect you."

"I never believed it either," CG McKinney said.

"I reckon," Richard Harden said without looking at Edgar, "that all us Hardens were always of a mind that Mister Watson was a good neighbor and was also good for the community. If DD House had of stayed home that day I reckon Chokoloskee and Everglades would be much better off as a place for our kin to live."

"Well," DD House almost yelled, "Y'all already made up your minds to beautify this crook and make him a saint, so I'm leaving before I get sick to my stomach."

And with that said he whooshed through the door like he was trying to catch up with the Frenchman.

"Last time I looked," Ted said, "beautification was a catholic thing."

Richard Harden spoke, "Probably a new word he learned and thought it was for all religions. A lot of them House folks considered themselves sorta like saints."

A voice behind everyone said softly, "All them House folks were that way."

"Oh dear God," Hannah Smith squealed loudly as she rushed forward, "Green Waller, my darling. I didn't know you were here."

"Saw the energy pumping inside this place and was a bit curious."

Hannah rushed to him and laid her huge head onto his small delicate shoulder.

"Well," Edgar drawled out, "I didn't expect t'see you here, Green."

"Well boss," Green Waller drawled out even farther, "I ain't never helt no ill feelins t'ords you. I got drunk many times when you's away on business, but thet day I let them hogs o' yorn git in the mash n' git schnockered, and yer favorite was half et by a panther, was more'n most of the boss men I ever worked for woulda stood for. You's always good t'me n' Hannah too, boss." He just stood there silent then as Hannah held him and left her head on his shoulder.

"Green," Edgar said with pinched lips and squinting eyes, as we all remained silent, wondering what was coming next, "I never held no bad feelings t'ords you're Miss Hannah, but I got a bad temper," his grin was wide and a bit childish looking, "and you n' every other person who ever knew me, understood, that I flash like dry twigs and settle down just as quick."

Adolphus Santini shook his head, "I've stood behind modern day family members and watched some sorry TV shows, but ain't yet seen anything to beat this." He moved a short distance toward the door before turning, "I'm not gonna hang around and watch y'all start crying." Before he whooshed through the big wide door, Tom Brewer yelled, "Hold on, Adolphus, ahm fed plum up with this dang buncha crybabies too." Moments later the two men were gone.

"Good riddance," Ted Smallwood said loudly.

Erskine Thompson said softly, "I reckon we oughta hear what these folks," he nodded at the three ladies that came with Edgar, "have to say about what happened that day down at Edgar's plantation."

I was frantically scribbling notes, even though the pain in my chest had returned. I was hoping everything was about to wind up and we could all go our separate way— mine would be to my bunk.

"Well ladies," Mister Watson turned to his entourage of three, "y'all ready to tell these here local folks, and this writer who's gonna tell the world," he nodded at me, "the truth about what happened that day on my plantation?"

Sadie Smith, who was less timid than her smaller sister (by a hundred more pounds and four inches in height) stepped forward to say, "I ain't never knowed you sir, nor have I ever been one of your workers, but my little sister was, an once we both got together," she sorta grinned, "after we both had been dead a while that is, she tole me exactly what happened." She paused to look right at Edgar, who finally told her to go ahead.

"Well, gentlemen, Hannah was left there at Chatham Bend with Leslie Cox, Green Waller, an some nigra men who was supposed t'do whatever Leslie tole 'em, because he was the foreman when Mister Watson was gone off on business for a while. Leslie got leg-wobblin drunk an was being real mean-mouthed t'ords m'sister an Green. Now I gotta tell y'all that lil sis said Green was mad-crazy in love with her and she with him. He wouldn't let nobody say no bad things about sis, so when Leslie began his bad-mouthin at sis, Leslie tole that scoundrel to shut his damn mouth or he'd shut it for him." She looked at Hannah a moment and shook her giant head side-to-side before she continued. "That dern Leslie had a pistol under the table pointing at Green all the time, an he just pulled on the trigger. The blast knocked Green back a ways before he fell over a'holdin to his belly, so's t'keep his guts in. Leslie stood an leaned forward n' shot Green in the head, an then turned to Hannah, who had already run into the kitchen to grab her razor sharp double-edged axe. Had she not been so upset by seeing her lover kilt right in front of her, none of us would be here talkin about this today. She got holt of the axe an swung harder'n most men could, meaning to take that skunk's head clean off. But all she did was graze his shoulder when Leslie ducked, an buried the axe near to the handle in the door jamb. He flopped onto the floor, so my sister leaped over him an fled up the stairs to get some kinda weapon," she looked at Hannah again, "she don't remember what it was she's goin for, but before she got to the top stair he shot her. Leslie musta leaped back when over four hundred pounds of woman came tumbling down them stairs. Hannah tole me she was stunned but not so bad that she couldn't roll over an scream at the nasty devil. She looked straight in his evil eyes as he stepped closer and shot her again, and then again." Sadie Smith then leaned against the counter and just shook her big head.

Ted Smallwood stood and stepped away from the chair, "That the way it happened, Hannah?"

"Yessir," she said softly, "that's izactly how I died," she raised her head off his shoulder and looked at Green, "and that's izactly how Green died too."

Ted looked straight at the young Indian girl, "You're Mikasuki, aincha?"

"Yes," she said, still looking at Hannah and shaking her head of long black hair.

"Did you see any of what happened that night inside Mister Watson's home?"

"Nossir, I didn't. Leslie Cox had tied me up inside the shed, so he could come in and rape me whenever he wished. He came to me before any of the things happened inside the big house. After raping me, Leslie hit me in the head with a shovel until I was dead, and then he put a rope around my neck and pulled my body up. My soul was in the corner watching. He tied the end of the rope to a round ring sticking up out of the cement floor. He laid a box on the side so it would look like I hung myself. There were more rings, because that's where he tied up the black men for the night after they worked all day plowing and such to get ready to plant vegetable and cane. I heard shooting in the big house later. My soul did not know where to go, so I stayed close to the house. My people heard all the shooting and had come close, but stayed on the other side of the river. Later, I followed them as they left to return to their small village a short distance away. They all watched as Leslie and a black man dragged the big woman and the tall thin man to the small boat. Leslie held a gun on the black man and made him row. My people said the white man didn't go far. He made the black man tie heavy things on the dead people and throw them in the water. After they returned and got out of the boat, Leslie shot the black man. A little later they heard many more shots, but were afraid he might have seen them, so they returned to their village. I heard all they said while my soul was with them. They decided to move their village in case Leslie came looking, he would not find them. My people, me, and everyone around the big house knew that Leslie was crazy, so when one of the young braves that were told to watch the big house until the village was moved, saw the man in the big black hat and long coat," she pointed at Edgar and said, "him, return and shoot Leslie in the head, they were very glad, but decided it was best to move as far away from white men as they could, and my soul went with them." She stood silently looking from one man to the next and finally stopped when her eyes got to Ted.

After a long silent pause, Ted spoke. "Well, as far's I am concerned, Edgar that explains how they all died. We will never know why Leslie Cox did what he did, but the Indians usually cut right through all the horse poop and get to the truth. I reckon Leslie was just another crazy man. Danged shame that the prison he was sentenced to for life, years earlier, wasn't built secure enough to keep the crazies away from us." Ted looked at the people standing there a moment then said, "I don't know about the rest of you, but I'm heading back to my grave to get some badly needed rest."

I sat in my chair at the table in the west wing and watched as they all walked right through the big door at the porch end of the east wing. Big Hannah Smith and her man, Green Waller followed her sister Sadie through the door. The two lovers had their arms around each other as they went through.

I slowly walked to the front door, wishing I could also just walk through that big door like they did and then float down to my boat. After locking it behind me I very slowly and very carefully walked down the stairs.

By the time I got the entrance hatch up, and was down the stairs, I didn't have enough left to engage the bolts that locked the hatch. *I'll get this thing locked later, but I got to get in that bunk for a while.* When I was finally stretched out, I thought, *boy, I'm glad this ghost thing if finished. I'll finish editing tonight's notes when I get up, but I've gotta rest a while now, so this damn pain in my chest'll stop.*

I have no idea what time it was when I heard the noise. My eyes just popped open. It was darker than when I came inside. *Must not be a moon or stars out there. Probably an overcast sky with a rainstorm coming.* I lay there looking up at the darkness when I heard it.

"Heh, heh, heh, heh, heh."

I located my flashlight and fumbled around until I located the switch.

The beam was pointing straight into the red eyes of something that I had never seen before. My gasp of surprise was probably heard, if anyone was nearby. I heard rustling noises and moved the beam. There were more eyes, all the same red—a blazing kind of red. I could now make out their shape. Short ghastly little creatures. My heart began pounding.

"Heh, heh, heh, heh, heh."

My heart was pounding and felt like it had a hot knife shoved into it. I moved the beam toward the laugh.

"Heh, heh, heh, heh, heh, heh, hehehehehehehe hehehehehehehehehehehehe." Robert the Doll was up and standing amongst the hideous little demons. He was giggling like a school girl.

My heart pounded like a caged animal wanting out of its cage.

"Heh, heh, heh, heh, heh, heh, heh, heh, heh, hehehehe hehehehehehehehe."

The pain was unbearable. The light dropped from my hand. "Now you can die."

I heard Robert the Doll laughing, "Heh, heh, heh, heh, heh, heh, heh, heh, heh, heh."

I flipped on the kitchen lights. There was Robert sitting on that can again, but there was nothing else in sight.

Robert went out through the porthole screen again, just like before, when he saw me reaching for my gun.

I looked at the clock. *Almost five AM so I might as well get up and make a pot of coffee.*

After filling my cup I did my best to update the entries in this daily journal. There was still a half cup of coffee in the cup when I stood. I sat back down to add a line, *this damn chest pain is killing me,* I thought as I scribbled. *That's an odd way to put it. I'm gonna lay back down for a while.*

7

GHOST WRITER

I DROVE INTO VIKING COUNTRY AND PARKED MY little Toyota motorhome that I named Stubby when I cut about eight feet off of the rear.

My blind little 15 year old Jackrat (half Jack Russell-half Rat Terrier) and I were heading toward Key Largo to visit with one of my daughters and her family. Dandy and I had stopped on the way down and spent the weekend in Port St. Lucie with my other daughter.

At the last minute I decided to turn off onto the old Alligator Alley and a while later turn south on highway 29 that runs straight into Everglades City.

I jogged right at Billy Potter's Seafood Junction, one of the best all-around seafood restaurants in the area. Billy got out of the stone crab trapping business years earlier and built a big restaurant named The Oyster House, right at the edge of Everglades City just before the causeway toward Chokoloskee begins. But a while later Billy was offered too much money for it to refuse.

A short time later, Billy realized that he missed having the restaurant to go to each day and create new entrée delights for his customers. He was soon negotiating for a restaurant that had closed down years earlier.

Billy's new place is the first restaurant a visitor sees when they come into Everglades city. They can either turn right and drive around the small city's central oval, or turn left into the parking lot of The Seafood Junction.

Those who don't when they first arrive, inevitably return for lunch, and usually return for dinner. Billy's delightful food is part of the new Everglades City success that other new businesses enjoy. Visiting fishermen and traveling tourists alike know they'll always get great meals at his huge restaurant.

I drove west to the circle and went around it, then headed south across the causeway for four miles. Once we rounded the curve I could see what was once an island, but was now connected to Everglades city by a causeway built in the 50s,—to the chagrin of many old timers.

My wife Dottie (1932/2002) and I had lived here on Chokoloskee during the seventies and eighties while I was trying to break into the stone crab trapping business. We eventually boarded our plane and flew south to live in South America and Jamaica for a few years—all of which is explained in my bestselling book, Dark Caribbean.

I pulled into the driveway of the McMillin's. Gary was an old trapper friend from those early days. His wife, Lynn, is the granddaughter of Ted Smallwood, the pioneer who built the trading post only a few blocks away. Lynn reopened it as a museum about twenty-five years ago. She allows me to sign copies of my books there during winter, and also made room for me to put a small camping trailer on their property. I'm 77 now in 2012 and consider success not in terms of high piles of money, but rather having good friends to age among.

I sat there in Stubby (a pic of her is at the end of this) a while looking across the property toward the bay. Gary's 52' boat was sitting in its slip, so I knew he hadn't taken a charter out today. He got out of the trapping business a few years earlier and re-geared the boat to carry out visiting fishermen.

Lynn's car was in the driveway beside me. I looked at my watch and saw that it was almost noon. *Must both be here,* I thought.

After another five minutes I decided to go up the stairs and knock, but just as I was stepping out I saw Lynn on the steep stairs coming down. "Hi, Rick," she said and waved.

"Hi, Lynn."

"What're you doing here? Dandy still with you?" she asked with a wide smile.

"Heading to the Keys to visit with my daughter, and ole Dandy's still with me. We're then heading to Key West to see how Dick's doing. How's everything coming with your civil lawsuit against that guy who shut the trading post down?"

"Don't ask. I got more problems than an Irishman in a dry county. One problem I have right now maybe you can help me with."

"Sure, whadaya need?"

"A guy that writes for a fishing magazine asked if he could come here and write about ghosts," her eyes closed and her head leaned as she puckered her lips, "that're supposedly being seen regularly by certain people who believe in that stuff. He told me the project was gonna end on Sunday, and he'd come over Monday to let me know when he was heading back to Key West in his boat. It's Tuesday and he shoulda been here already. His boat has been docked right behind the trading post." Lynn's eyebrows went up, "He's about your age, but he's very heavy, so I hope everything's alright with him. I gotta be at the court house in Naples in a little over an hour, so can you go over and check on him. His name is Pyorrhea Lam."

"His dad a dentist," I said with a smile.

"Darned if I know," she answered with a smile.

"Go ahead to Naples and take your time, Lynn, and do whatever y'gotta do to beat that little creep who shutcha down. I'll check on the guy n' letcha know when you get back here."

Before Dandy and I left here in May the road had already been dug up and a fence was installed all the way around the property that guy had purchased, including the old motel on the corner that Lynn's dad built many years ago. There was no way to get to the trading post except to walk through the swamp on a small trail that someone, kids most likely, made years earlier, probably to go there to fish.

If the tide was in, you had a foot of water in some places, but all the way across to the road it was still a few inches deep.

I got lucky, because someone carried in a few bags of a type of shredded mulch, and put it on the deeper areas. So it wasn't too bad as long as I was careful where I put my shoeless hoofs. Dandy just walked along on the leash until he had to swim a little to get back up on the high ground. His short legs can't handle deep water.

Once I got to a section of Mamie Drive I removed the sneakers from around my neck and untied 'em. Walking now on asphalt in shoes, I was soon at the dock looking at this guy, Pyorrhea's boat. I had already tied Dandy's leash to a water pipe, so I walked along the dock looking for a door but never found one. I leaned out and hammered on the roof with my fist. After three tries I stood back to see if the boat moved, because Lynn said he was a hefty fella.

When I noticed that the boat didn't move at all, I stepped on. Holding to the rail attached to the roof, I walked to the small deck on the bow. I leaned over and tried to see through the front window but immediately saw that it had a plastic shield on it. I used it to cover all of the windows on my offshore crawfishing boat that I cruised the Caribbean with when a pal and I carried crawfishing traps on our two boats as we searched the Caribbean for places to set 'em.

Still holding to the handrail I bent down to look in at each small porthole—no easy feat for an old fart that would pass life's Mile Marker 77 on June 30th.

The portholes were all open but the screens made it difficult to see much. I spotted the steering wheel and a nice looking Captain's Chair. I went to the next one and looked in. I could see a porthole on the starboard side and there was nothing in between. The third one was the same, which must have allowed a nice breeze to pass through the forward section of the boat. The fourth one was above a sink, and as my eyes adjusted to looking through screen I spotted the guy.

"Hey Pyorrhea," I yelled loudly but never saw him move. Yelling two more times got no movement either, so I slowly stood up and waited a moment for my back to stop yelling nasty expletives.

I carefully walked along to the stern, and thought I'd located the entry door, but it didn't take me long to realize that this hatch wasn't the entry. *Locked on the inside,* I thought, *this is probably the engine room.*

I noticed the propane bottles earlier but didn't pay any attention to 'em because I carried mine on the roof of my boat too, so they'd be outa the way and easy to get on n' off when they needed filling.

But now that I was standing beside them I could see a hatch that had to be the entry. As I hefted m'self up to the top I thought, *If this guy locked this hatch after he went in to take a nap'r som'n, I'm gonna hafta call the Everglades City Fire Department to bring their Jaws of Life to get it open.*

I held my breath as I put my fingers under the lip and lifted. I breathed easy as it came up with little effort. I saw the ladder still in the down position as I held the attached rope, obviously put there to allow the hatch to go back until it was leaning against a crossbar that separated the bottles from the hatch.

My admiration for whoever designed and built this boat was going up. I yelled down into the main salon, but when I got my first whiff of the air inside, I stood up and took in a deep breath of fresh air.

For one reason or another, I've been around a few not so fresh cadavers, so I left the hatch up and used my cell phone to call the Sheriff's Department in EC.

I was sitting in the shade petting Dandy when they arrived. After telling them why I was there and why I had opened the hatch, two of them went down the ladder.

On Thursday a call from the Sheriff's sub-station at the corner of Tamiami Trail and the road into Everglades City asked me to come and give a statement.

After I signed the statement an older fella with stripes on his sleeve…a sergeant I reckon, came over and checked it out. He was satisfied, and then told me that the county coroner had already determined that it was a massive heart attack. "You or Lynn can go on the boat now and clean up or do whatever is needed."

I thanked him and headed back to Chokoloskee. Later in the day, Lynn was home so I pulled in and walked up the stairs. I knew she'd be there at her computer because I called earlier to let her know I was going to the substation to give a statement.

After explaining everything to her, Lynn said, "I called the editor that Py was writing for during his writing life, and he told me to ask you to call him. I told him you had written several books and was signing copies here at the trading post. He said that he'd been putting out hints on Facebook about the book on ghosts that Py had been working on, and his readers are anxious to read some excerpts in his magazine so they can decide whether or not to buy the book. Might not be a bad idea to edit his notes and publish it yourself."

"Yeah, it's worth looking into. I'll look around in the boat and find his notes. You got that editor's number?"

With the number in my cell phone, I left and headed toward the path through the swamp again. After parking Stubby where I parked it before, I put Dandy on his leash and headed through the water toward the trading post.

Dandy is blind and didn't seem to mind the water. He's been with me fifteen years and the last three, his eyesight has progressively gotten worse. A while back he was diagnosed with diabetes—about four years I think. I've given him a shot of insulin morning and evening ever since. He's a great little companion and I don't mind atol being his seeing-eye-people.

I tied him to the same water pipe and headed down the stairs to look for the guy's note book. When I spotted it on the food tray attachment that was added to his Captain's chair, I climbed up and sat down.

After going quickly through it I realized that he either had a helluva good imagination or there had been some real ghostly things going on up in the trading post.

I put the notebook down and called his editor in Miami.

Twenty-five minutes later we had worked out a deal—in between the calls that caused him to put me on hold. He was a very busy guy, but sounded like he knew what he was doing. Through research that I was getting pretty good at, I later learned that his dad had started that magazine forty-some years earlier and now sent over two hundred thousand copies to cash subscribers every two months.

He would fax Lynn a contract for me to write the book and publish it through my publishing company, Grizzly Bookz Publishing. The deal he accepted was 75% for me and 25% for his magazine after all printing costs. A clause would state that I would send an excerpt within two weeks so he could post it to his paid subscribers on his magazine's website, and then another in a month.

I told Lynn that I'd better get to work on those notes. I stopped before opening her door, and turning, I asked, "Do you think it would be alright if I stay on his boat a while to work on the manuscript?"

"Sure, if you're not scared of ghosts and stuff like that. His editor said it'll be a while before he'll have a friend of Py's come get the boat. You oughta be able to stay there and be comfortable, because he has it plugged in with an extension cord so his batteries'll stay up without running his generator too much."

"Great, because Dandy'll be able to stay on a long leash between those poles, and I won't hafta worry about him falling off the dock."

"He fell off the seawall over here last winter, didn't he?"

"Yeah, he fell in the water but somehow worked his way to the end where he was able to get out. I opened the door at about ten at night and there he was. Soaked and all scarred up from the oysters he'd climbed across, but otherwise he was okay. That ended his freedom, though.

I've been keeping him on a leash ever since. I made him a long steel line between two cypress trees up at Larry and Beth's place, but I've still gotta figure out some way to rig up a steel line here for him to move back and forth on."

"Okay," Lynn said, turning back to her computer. "Stop by and lemme know how everything's going."

"Reckon you'll get the road put back by the time those Snowbuzzards show up?"

"I'm sure trying hard to get the court to force him to replace the one he dozed out."

"Good luck." I headed down the stairs.

By the end of the first day, I had read all of his notes. I plugged in my computer to another extension cord that I brought from the cabin we spend the summer in at my pal Larry's place up in North Florida. His wife Beth is the daughter of an old friend of mine from Naples. Sadly he died of cancer a few years ago. Beth and Larry look after me n' Dandy like we're family. The property is way off the beaten path, and we all love it that way.

A week of fifteen hour days at the computer, I not only had both excerpts done and ready to send, but I was on the last quarter of Py's notes.

I knew that I would have to edit everything a few times, and then have friends that I trust to critique the entire manuscript and tell me the truth. After reading their suggestions and correcting typos, then I would read it one last time before printing the book.

My Aussie Webmaster is a good artist who created a cover for my book, Blue Water Adventure, retitled Dark Caribbean because so many people looked at the cover and thought it was about a couple of guys going out to catch some 'little fishies', as I heard one old guy say. Once the potential reader turned the book over to read the rear cover, they knew immediately that it wasn't. But I had seen so many people pass on by after seeing that beautiful cover that I decided to have a new one created. It worked because sales shot up and the book's still one of the best selling books in the Smallwood Trading Post. I've donated all proceeds from copies of Dark Caribbean sold there each season to the trading post.

I plowed ahead during the next three or four days and completed transferring Py's notes into the manuscript. It was only seven o'clock and not yet getting dark, so I got the rewinding leash and took Dandy for a long walk. We went through the swamp on the path and I realized then how dark it was in there, so I was glad I had thought to bring my flashlight. We walked to the corner about two city blocks away, and then turned back. Once we were beneath the trading post I took my time so Dandy could have one last pee. He drinks four times the water that a dog without diabetes does, and has a bladder about the size of a water buffalo, so I make sure he's emptied it before taking him inside.

Sure enough he dumped about a pint in three different places. After giving him enough time to poop again if needed, which he didn't, because he'd already left his calling card in the roadside weeds, I carried him on the boat and then down the ladder.

I'd already fed him and given him his evening shot of insulin, so after giving Dandy his evening few dollops of ice cream—screw the diabetes, I made him comfortable on a pillow that I knew Py would never need again.

It was dark now, so I turned on one light and then opened my computer. I returned to the editing that I had started and worked until about midnight. Something seemed out of sync, so I thumbed through the last few pages of his notes. Still trying to figure out what it was, I went through those last two pages again, and as I went to close the notebook, the last page I had looked at folded up a bit, from the fan I figured then, but now I don't know?

Anyway I spotted writing; actually it appeared to me as scribbling by someone in a terrible hurry.

After reading those hurried notes that Py, or someone, or something, had somehow scribbled on the last page of the notebook—a page incidentally that had absolutely nothing on it, because it was the only blank page, and I started to write something on it but changed my mind.

I wondered if somehow Py was one of those rare people that can see ghosts and communicate with them. Below is what I found scribbled on that page when I returned from walking Dandy last night.

~ O ~

By the time I got the entrance hatch up, and was down the stairs, I didn't have enough energy left to engage the bolts that locked the hatch. I'll get that thing locked later, but I've gotta get into that bunk. Finally stretched out, I thought, boy, I'm glad this ghost thing if finished. I'll finish editing tonight's notes when I get up, but I've gotta rest a while now, so this damn pain in my chest'll stop.

I have no idea what time it was when I heard the noise. My eyes just popped open. It was darker than when I came inside. Must not be a moon or stars out there. Probably a rainstorm coming. I lay there looking up at the darkness when I heard it.

Heh, heh, heh, heh, heh.

I located my flashlight and fumbled around until I located the switch.

The beam was pointing into the red eyes of something I'd never seen before. I heard rustling noises and moved the beam. There were more frightening eyes, all the same—a blazing kind of blood-red. I could now make out their shape. Short little creatures. My heart began pounding.

Heh, heh, heh, heh, heh.

I moved the beam toward the laugh. Heh, heh, heh, heh, heh, heh, hehehehehehehehehehehe. Robert the Doll was standing amongst the hideous little demons and giggling like a school girl. My heart pounded like an animal wanting out of its cage. Heh, heh, heh, heh, heh, heh, heh, heh, heh, heh, hehehehehehehehehehehe.

The pain was unbearable, so I laid back down on the bed. The light dropped from my hand. Now you can die, Robert the Doll said one last time.

It was the last thing I would ever hear—everything suddenly went black.

A note from the author:

Cap Watson was the name of a friend of my father, Murl Magers. Later, when Cap lived on a houseboat behind Pedro's Boatyard in Tavernier, Florida, a short ride south of Key Largo, my wife Dottie and I became close friends with the old mariner. We lived aboard our yacht at Pedro's, but in a secure slip with pilings to tie onto, and a dock to walk from the car to the boat.

Shortly before WW-II ended, Cap was building a small sloop at the American Yacht Basin at Flagler Street and the Miami River. Murl Magers, his wife, Betty, and their son, Richard—me, (renamed Rick in the early 60s by Dottie) lived aboard an old houseboat at the same place. Murl walked over one day and spoke to Cap. "Hello, I watched as you set up everything to build a boat. Even though I've never built one, maybe I can give you a hand when you need one."

It led to a friendship that lasted a half-century.

Many years later in Tavernier, a key just south of Key Largo, Cap Watson was helping a friend get his houseboat secured prior to an approaching storm. It was in the 1980s, and turned out to be a bit too much for a man 103 years old. Cap was buried a few days later.

A few months earlier Cap had told Dottie and I a story that fits in with this book, so I'll tell it here as he told it to us.

Cap leaned back into the plush easy-chair on his small but roomy houseboat moored in the basin behind Pedro's

Boatyard in Tavernier. "Rick," he asked, "have you heard about a guy named Mister Watson who started farming sugarcane at Chatham Bend, a place along the coast, west of Flamingo?"

"Nope, doesn't ring a bell, Cap." (I have since read several books by Peter Matthiessen, including Shadow Country, which is the complete book about Mister Watson; how he lived, and why the people living on Chokoloskee Island killed him.)

"I don't know if the story's true that he really killed his hired help rather than pay them, but it's a fact that those folks on Chokoloskee Island gunned him down, because they believed he did. It happened right there beneath the Smallwood Trading Post."

"Wow," I said, "those are not the kind of people to push."

"I always stopped to stock up on provisions at Ted Smallwood's Trading Post whenever I sailed over to Everglades City to visit friends," Cap said. "I knew Ted Smallwood quite well and never knew the man to tell a lie or even stretch the truth. He didn't believe Mister Watson killed his hired help rather than pay them their wages."

One day when just Ted and I were in the trading post he said, "Cap, Edgar was a very bright fella, and he knew that hired help down here at the end of the world was hard to come by. Even if there had been plenty of people to hire, I still don't believe he woulda done som'n like that."

Cap took a sip of the fresh key limeade that he had made just prior to us tying beside him. It reminded Dottie about the ten pounds of sugar we bought in Islamorada before pointing the boat toward Tavernier. "Hold the story, Cap," Dottie said, "I'll get the sugar we bought you."

With the sugar stashed in the cabinet, Cap continued. "All o' them Chokoloskee boys were armed and waiting down by the water for him to come in and surrender. At least that's the way I heard it. No matter what actually caused 'em to be armed n' ready, Mister Watson was not a man to be rubbed the wrong way. Listen to this story, Rick, and you'll understand why I lied to him on the one and only time we met, even though he was only a ghost by then."

Cap poured himself a small glass of rum, and offered each of us one, but we refused. Whenever we returned from a cruise aboard the 40' Huckins we lived aboard, we put her beside Cap's houseboat that was moored a hundred yards out from Pedro's building. First we'd give him a bottle of rum and a few of whatever we caught, including his very favorite, crawfish tails—which I could always dive up or get from the ice cans that I had carried out a year earlier.

Then Dottie and I would sit inside his boat and listen with rapt attention to his stories for a while. This was the best that Cap ever told us.

"Rick, Dottie, I can tell you for a fact that Mister Watson was one scary guy when you got up close to him. I had heard about him killing the workers that helped him grow sugar cane, when they demanded he give them some of their payday money. It always sounded kinda far-fetched t'me, and was reinforced by Ted Smallwood feeling the same way, as did many others who had known him or worked for him. For safety's sake though, every time I left Flamingo and was sailing toward Everglades City and Chokoloskee, I made a point of going way out so I would pass Chatham Bend a few miles offshore." Cap twisted the top off the rum and poured himself another shot of rum, then grinned at both of us. "Y'never know what kind of foolishness a bunch of ghosts might be up to."

"I built that small sloop," he looked at me, "the one your daddy helped me with, Rick," Cap continued, "to cruise the Bahamas. I made it so I could crank up the steel keel and pull down a little canvas if I was in shallow water.

Well now, on this particular day, I was in good water about five miles off Chatham Bend, when I saw a puff of smoke inshore of me. There was barely enough breeze to keep the sail from flapping, so it wasn't long before I saw another puff of smoke.

To this very day I don't know why, but I knew it was Edgar Watson's boat, and he was heading straight toward me. My boat was barely making headway, so wasn't long before I could actually see his hull."

Cap looked at me then turned toward Dottie. "This was back in 1950 and Edgar Watson was gunned down on Chokoloskee Island in 1910." Cap just shook his head slowly.

"My mind was racing, because I was just a young feller and scared half to death. He was purposely running me down, because black smoke was pouring out of his single exhaust stack, which I could also now easily see. I was thinking, *what the heck am I gonna do?—why is he running me down?—is he taking all available help that he comes to, back to his plantation at gunpoint? Can ghosts shoot guns?* My mind raced.

Before I could get some reasonable answers to all the crazy questions running through my mind, Mister Watson was pulling alongside. I had already dropped the sail, so I took that line he offered and tied it to a cleat.

He had a wide friendly smile across his face when he pulled the cigar from his mouth. Holding it out, I could see that it wasn't lit, and he spoke in a soft and very easy manner.

'I never leave the dock without at least two boxes of matches,' he said, 'so what do I do today?' His smile turned to a sheepish grin as his lips puckered and his cheeks pulled in, 'Went t'light this damn thing,' he lifted the cigar again, 'and about that time I stepped on a loose floorboard and twisted my ankle.' He shoved it back in his mouth and did a funny kinda nod with his head, 'caught myself before I fell outa the damn boat, but the whole box o' matches,' he grinned, 'the only damn one I brought today, was in the water n' floatin away. I started to jump in n' get 'em, but then I thought about all the bull sharks in this area.' He grinned again, 'I just stood there like a big dummy n' watched that damn box o' matches float away.'

He looked pleadingly at me, 'I hope you have a spare box that I can buy from you, neighbor, because I'm on my way to Key West with a load of my cane syrup, and I'm already running a bit late.'

I kept control of myself so he wouldn't hear the big sigh of relief that wanted badly to burst through my lips. A big smile erupted across my mug instead. "I have a coupla boxes wrapped in oilcloth," I said, as I scooted into my little cabin. "**Here they are**," I said loudly from inside.

After getting back into my stern cockpit, I handed him a full box of matches. "I whacked off a chunk of oilcloth that you can wrap 'em in so they'll stay dry," I said, and passed it to him then leaned back against a cushion.

After carefully removing one match, he raised it as if to light the cigar, but there was still no fire or smoke. Mister Watson then wrapped up the box thoroughly. After stashing the box of matches in a tin lard can that he retrieved from the bow beneath a small decked area, he returned and stood there puffing on the unlit cigar for a moment." Cap shook his head of white hair slowly back and forth before continuing, "I could see that it wasn't lit, but sure wasn't gonna say anything. Later on I learned that he had an unlit cigar in his mouth when he was shot."

'Neighbor,' Mister Watson said after removing the unlit cigar and holding it aloft to admire the end, 'you saved my life today.'

Mister Watson blew out air as though it was a cloud of smoke that would make both of our boats invisible. He then dug around in his pocket and came up with a handful of change.

'How much do I owe you for the matches?'

"Wow," Dottie said, "betcha felt good when y'learned all he wanted was matches."

"I sure was, and seeing that shotgun everyone said he always had with him, lying right there on a seat in his cockpit, I was hoping he would be moving on. I told him to accept the matches as a gift from one mariner to another."

After puffing up the unlit cigar he put the coins back in his pocket and held out his hand. He spoke around the cigar, 'That's right neighborly, thank you.' As I shook his hand he said, 'My name's Watson, what's yours?'

Without batting an eye I answered, "Jones, pleased t'meetcha, Mister Watson."

'My pleasure, Mister Jones, my pleasure indeed. If you sail by one day, stop in for a visit with me at my farm on Chatham Bend and I'll be glad to fill your larder with fresh vegetables and a quart jar of my sugarcane syrup.' He shoved away and smiled wide, 'Best damn syrup you'll ever put on your flapjacks, Mister Jones'. Watson waved, 'I gotta get movin now, good sailing to you, sir.'

"I waved and waved until he was a fair piece west, and then I flopped down in the cockpit and let some energy seep back into my legs. Even after a good pull from my bottle of rum I was still weak-kneed and wobbly, so I took my time raising the mainsail."

"Boy Cap," Dottie said, "that was quick thinking."

"Yessiree," Cap'n Watson grinned, and then sipped his rum. "My brain was much younger back then and more pliable. I was constantly surprising myself back in those days." He chuckled, "I wasn't about to tell a potential killer named Mister Watson that my name is Captain Watson."

About other books by this author

- **Dark Caribbean**…is based on a true story. Offshore lobstermen battle pirates for years, and eventually begin smuggling drugs. Airplanes, airboats, 150 mph pickemup trucks, gunfire, riding alligators, wild men, wilder women—it's all in this one…and it's all true.
- **The McKannahs**…is a western adventure novel that begins in 17th century Ireland and moves to early 18th century America. 5 McKannah sons and 1 daughter spread out across this wild new country to build their life.
- **The McKannahs ~together again~** … the four McKannah brothers come to Montana and stand with Jesse as he confronts men intent on wiping out his Flathead Indian friends. Their sister, Aleena…well, she……….
- **Carib Indian**…this is the only novel written specifically about these courageous freedom fighters. Holding wooden spears in their hand-carved canoes, they took on mighty ships full of modern soldiers that had entered the Caribbean Sea in search of slaves.
- **The Face Painter**…is a book of stories for young readers 8 to 88.
- **The Black Widowmaker**…was a beautiful black woman who made widows of many women, but after reading her story, you might find yourself sympathizing with her.
- **Satan's Dark Angels**…is a collection of frightening stories, and now it accompanies The Black Widowmaker…making 2 novellas in 1 book.
- **America**…is a book of western and other short stories.

- **A Sacred Vow**...My Memoir.
- **It's A Dog's Life**...the author's 15 year old, blind, ½ Jack Russell- ½ Rat terrier — Jack-Rat, always wanted to write his autobiography. With help from Rick he finally finished it. All proceeds go to homeless animal caregivers, most recently, Freeway Petey the Greyhound.
- **80 Stories**...is great for folks who don't like to face one long story in a novel. You'll find almost every genre in this one. Sad, funny, unbelievable, maddening, frightening, whacky, true, thought-provoking, award winning and some you will read over-and-over.
- **Ladybug and the Dragon**...is the true story of Tampa native, Katia Solomon. At 2 she was diagnosed with leukemia. Rather than write a story about her, as he was asked to do by a magazine editor, Rick decided to write a small book and send the Solomon family all of the money from sales to assist them during that difficult time. Katia turned 12 in 2012 and remains in remission, but now they are about to have their small house re-possessed. It's the one her mama was raised in, and Katia loves. Rick updated the book in an effort to save their home.

Go to his website **www.grizzlybookz.net** to learn how to order a copy signed by Katia, so she can stay in the home she loves.....................*Thanks*

Uninvited...Coming in Fall 2013. Go to page 210 to read more.

SMALLWOOD STORE

HISTORIC
OLE INDIAN TRADING POST
and MUSEUM

Established in 1906, the Smallwood Store & Trading Post served the area with a place to trade hides, furs and farm produce; handle mail and to sell needed goods to the settlers. It is now a museum and gift shop telling the history of southwest Florida.

OPEN 7 DAYS A WEEK
December – April
10:00 a.m. - 5:00 p.m.

May – November
11:00 a.m. – 5:00 p.m.

(239) 695-2989
(239) 695-4454 Fax
P.O. Box 310
Chokoloskee, Florida 34138
Web Site: www.smallwoodstore.com

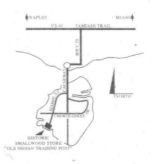

STUBBY

My copilot and traveling companion, Dandy.

**Printed by Americans in the USA
at
Snowfall Press**

~ O ~

Don't miss Rick's next book.

AVAILABLE

Fall 2013

--- O ---

UNINVITED

Will the wildlife in the

one-and-only Everglades on this

wonderful Blue Planet be only a memory

by 2040 — or will the authorities listen to the

men who know how many are out there

and how to eliminate them before

it is too late?

Read a little about it on the next page.

One last look around, and then he listened for noise that did not belong...Charlie Potter slowly lifted his head up above the mound he had just come to...His eyes were not ready for what he saw·

1

FOURTEEN-YEAR-OLD JEREMY SLIPPED QUIETLY OUT the back door of his fathers' hunting cabin.

After two years of heated arguing, his mother had given in and allowed him to board a plane in New Jersey and spend part of the summer with his father in Naples, Florida.

The ride in his father's airboat filled the boy's mind with re-runs of Wild Kingdom. "We're gonna spend the whole week out in the Everglades?"

"Yep," his father answered, "bout time you see the real side of life—a real man's world." His smile thrilled the short, pale, ninety-pound young boy.

The first day at the small cabin, Emmitt brought out the new Remington .22 rifle and handed it to Jeremy. "I think it's time you have your own rifle, son."

Jeremy stood transfixed with his mouth hanging open and

his eyes stretched wide as he held a gun for the very first time.

"It's not loaded, but don't point it at anything, because so-called unloaded guns have killed lots of amateurs. "I'm gonna teach you how to load it, clean it, shoot it, and the can-dos and no-can-dos."

A quart bottle of Jack Daniels sat on the table next to a small Igloo of ice cubes. Emmitt filled his glass. After a long sip, he opened the fresh box of ammunition and put his heart into teaching his son how to load, shoot, and care for his first gun...between sips of JD.

By the time the sun was approaching the tops of the western trees, Jeremy had filled several targets with holes and was feeling more confidence than at any other point in his short life.

Standing less than four feet tall, Jeremy had become a devout mama's boy and the bait for every bully in the school. His mother had divorced Emmitt when Jeremy was five. They moved to New Jersey to be near her parents. Between them and Jeremy's over-protective mother, the young boy had been sheltered from everything that makes a boy a boy. He had never been exposed to the basic essentials that prepares a boy for eventual manhood.

The second day began at noon when his father took a short pull from the second bottle of Jack Daniels. After he swished it around in his mouth, he swallowed and let the warmth flow through his body. "Ahhhhh," he crooned as he swung his short legs out from beneath the mosquito netting. After revolving his head several times, he shook off the JD cobwebs, lifted the net, and shoved it behind so he could stand.

After scooping two strawberry yogurts into his still cotton-lined maw, he looked at his son. Jeremy was sitting on the wide windowsill with his feet hanging outside. "Didja have some breakfast, son?"

"Yessir," he turned and smiled at his father, "fixed myself a big bowl of Special-K."

"That's good, son, gotta start each day with a full belly." Emmitt walked to the nearest window and looked at the sky, and then scanned the hammock he had built the cabin in. "We'll go out later this afternoon and see if we can shoot a coupla Chokoloskee chickens for dinner."

"What are chuckleiskee chickens?"

"Curlew," Emmitt answered, "actually they're ibis, a local native bird that's a lot better eatin than them store-bought, force-fed buzzards them stores're sellin as chickens." He grinned at his son who grinned back, even though he had no idea what his dad was talking about. The only food he had ever seen, except restaurant food, was either packaged, frozen, or in a can.

Afternoon came and then went out with the second empty whiskey bottle. Jeremy listened to Emmitt ramble on about his hard times, with no used cars selling—fuel to go out in his airboat being so high he couldn't use it very often—what a bitch Jeremy's mother was—how she'd ruined his life, etc., etc. After a few more complaints, he started at the beginning again.

That's when Jeremy said he was too tired and went into his bedroom. He sat staring into the dark hammock, dreaming of alligators, panthers, bobcats, and all the other animals that his father had filled his dreams with each time during the past year when the boy called him.

Jeremy suffered through another day of waiting for his father to get up and take him into the swamp. When Emmitt drank himself into a stupor and fell asleep in the old recliner, Jeremy went to his room and began putting together the things he would need to go hunting when the sun came up.

The following morning Jeremy waited until he was far away from the cabin and deep into the dense hammock before he sat down in a clearing and got out a peanut butter and jelly sandwich. After wadding the paper bag and shoving it beneath a fallen tree trunk, he washed down the last of the sandwich with a cold Pepsi. He then pulled out the box of .22 caliber shells to fill his very own Remington pump-action rifle.

With the tube full of bullets, he pumped one into the chamber, exactly as his father had taught him. Jeremy then checked to be certain that the safety was on, just as he was told to do—between Jack Daniels breaks.

3

*F*IFTY-FIVE MILES AWAY IN A NORTH NAPLES CLUB named The Village Lounge, a pair of dark complexioned men wearing very expensive silk suits, Gucci shoes, and mirrored designer sunglasses, sat in an isolated private booth talking.

"Everything going okay?" The swarthy man with the gold rimmed shades said.

Jerome Sennitt smiled, "Sure is, Amad. My people in Miami are anxious to see the product, and if it's as pure as you say, they'll be able to pay cash for any amount you can supply them with."

"Very good," the other man replied.

Both men were six-footers and very powerfully built. Four meetings with the two men and Jerome still felt an evil power radiating from them.

"Jerome," the first man said, "your wife's family that still lives in Cuba is extremely well connected." He took a brief sip of his apricot brandy cocktail before speaking again. "My associate," he nodded at the man sitting across from him, "Jintan, has family in Havana, and they know them quite well even though they have never done business together." He leaned back in his plush captain's chair to fish out a thin black cigarette from his solid gold case.

When Jerome had met them through one of his wife's cousins, three months earlier, he mentally separated them as Mister Gold and Mister Silver. Amad had gold frames on his dark glasses, gold cufflinks, gold tie pin, a gold case where he kept his foul-smelling cigarettes, a gold Rolex, and a gold money-clip.

Jintan had silver duplicates of everything that Amad exposed for Jerome to see. He chuckled to himself when he was alone following this fifth meeting with the two mysterious men. *I'll bet*, he thought, *they carry condoms with gold and silver rims.*

"His people in Cuba told him that they can be trusted." Amad turned toward Mister Silver, "Isn't that right, Jintan?"

"Yessir, they are well known in the business circles my family moves in, and all say they are solid reliable people to do business with."

The entire time he spoke, Jerome had the feeling that Mister Silver was simply repeating something that he had memorized, and was working hard to bring the words forward.

Mister Gold leaned slightly forward, "Jerome, we have checked you out thoroughly and are very pleased with the results. The attache case I carried in this time has two hundred thousand dollars in it for you to move ahead now and begin setting up the operation we discussed. It also has a half kilo of our product for you to show your people." He lifted the small round glass to his lips while watching Jerome. When he sat the glass down, Mister Gold said, "We will leave now, but will remain in the car down the street to be sure you are not followed." He smiled for the first time since they had met, and Jerome saw that his two eye teeth were gold. "We'll meet at number six on your list in four weeks. We'll then see how everything is progressing."

The two men stood, and Mister Silver placed a pair of twenties on the table to cover the two cocktails and the beer that Jerome drank half of.

4

FORTY-FIVE MILES EAST, TWO YOUNG BOYS FROM Miami Springs, Hialeah's sister city on the south side of the Miami River, were moving across the sawgrass in a new airboat. It was a sixteen foot long fiberglass hull, and was powered by a Porche air-cooled Engine. It had a four-blade composit propellar, and ingnoring Ronnies plea to leave the straight pipes on the Engine, his father had mufflers installed.

"There's enough noise in this new world, son, so we'll not add to it."

Ronnie Weingarten's wealthy father had promised to buy him an airboat on his eighteenth birthday. A month earlier it was delivered to their ten acre estate, The Weingarten Garden.

Ronnie completed a two-day course in Air Boat Safety at a man-made swamp ten miles north of his home. His entire life had been filled with toys—battery-powered sportscars, trucks, forklifts, and motorbikes all went to the dump soon after Ronnie climbed on his first gasoline powered Honda dirt bike.

His sixteenth birthday party ended with Ronnie and his lifetime best friend, Ziggy Skatze, taking turns riding around the oval course with rolling hills that were created just for the dirtbike. The other 30+ guests were ignored.

His seventeenth birthday eclipsed all others when he saw the brand new 2019 Dodge Magnum-*PLUS* pickup truck being delivered on a flatbed. The white silk ribbon and bow on top made the black metalic paint seem to shimmer even more.

"I had the brake pedal modified," his five-foot-tall father said, "exactly like I did mine, and the accelerator too. You can adjust the seat and reach 'em just fine."

The Ram had towed the airboat to the launch ramp in west Hialeah. The two boys parked the truck and trailer beside five other truck/trailers that had already shed their airboats. Those men were already out roaring across the sawgrass. Ronnie removed his regular shoes, and pulled on his leather, custom--built 5" elevated boots. He bought them at Jorge Gonzalez' Safari Outfitters in the Hialeah Mall. The moment he pulled them on, he thought, *the best eight hundred bucks I ever spent.*

Ronnie flipped on his theft alert, which would summon a helicopter once they saw his father's name on the alert. One last look inside to be sure he hadn't left anything, and Ronnie locked the truck and swaggered toward Ziggy, who was holding the bowline. Two short boys feeling better in each other's presence—one now five inches taller.

Ronnie climbed up to the seat sitting on top of a six-foot high aluminum frame. After starting the Engine, he nodded to Ziggy, who coiled the rope and climbed in. He had driven his father's friend, their next-door neighbor Bill's, airboat a few times when he was invited to ride along with him. Mister Hobart pointed out some of the ways a driver can get into a serious situation with an airboat. Ronnie listened intently whenever the old man spoke—he figured Mister Hobart was wise, because he was old like his father, who was thirty-eight.

Ziggy had the mental apparatus of a twelve-year-old. He continuously held his arm up motioning for Ronnie to go faster. Ronnie loved speed, whether on his dirt bike, in his truck, or driving across the sawgrass like now. However, when he felt the urge to bump the airboat throttle ahead a bit, he recalled Mister Hobart's words, and left it alone.

When Ziggy dug a Coke from the ice chest, Ronnie tapped him on the shoulder with the toe of his $800 Tony Lama, lizard skin, elevated jungle boots. Watching where he was going, Ronnie held his hand out while he opened and closed it a few times.

Ziggy yelled, "What?" several times before Ronnie put his

hand to his lips as though drinking. "Oh," Ziggy yelled, and dug a Coke out of the ice and handed it up.

One hour later, Ronnie pulled the throttle back as he eased the boat toward a large hammock.

"You been to this one before, Ronnie?"

"Nope."

"We gonna tie up n' see if we can find us a few of those pythons?"

"Yeah, but I'm gonna idle around it and see if there's a better place to tie up and scout around inside this hammock."

Ronnie located a spot where the nose of the boat would ease in far enough for them to step off onto dry land.

Once the boat was secured to the mangroves, Ronnie said, "Strap your machete on tight, Ziggy, and secure the rawhide tong at the bottom of the sheath to your leg so it doesn't flop around." He watched Ziggy as he strapped on his own machete and then secured it to his leg. "Yeah man, that looks good. You carry the sacks and I'll bring the loop-stick I built."

Ziggy watched as Ronnie untied the lines that held the six-foot-long aluminum tubing that he had fashioned into a snake lariat after one he saw on Animal Kingdom.

"Hold your arm out, Ziggy, so I can test this, one last time before we go after 'em."

His friend complied, and Ronnie reached out with the loop-stick. The 3/16th inch stainless steel cable looped over Ziggy's wrist easily. The other ends of the cable were clamped to a round wooden handle, so all he had to do was pull on the handle while holding the aluminum tube, and the coil snugged up to Ziggy's wrist.

"Pretty cool, man." Ziggy said as he admired his best friend's invention. When the loop was removed, Ziggy put on his new African Safari White Hunter canvas jungle hat, and watched as his friend adjusted his. Ziggy had an unlimited debit card, so he'd bought each of them one of the $189.99 hats.

Ronnie had bought himself a pair of $150 Oakley Polarized Frogskin Sunglasses, so Ziggy bought a pair too.

They stepped out of the boat looking like two kids on a Sesame Street Safari.